Gatherings

Recipes from Montana's Mustang Kitchen

Carole Sullivan

Photographs by Lynn Donaldson

Graphic Design by Engine 8

Edited by Seabring Davis

Food Styling by Carole Sullivan

ISBN 10: 1-59152-132-7

ISBN 13: 978-1-59152-132-7

Published by Carole Sullivan

You may order extra copies of this book by calling Farcountry Press
toll free at (800) 821-3874.

Produced by Sweetgrass Books.

PO Box 5630, Helena, MT 59604; (800) 821-3874;

www.sweetgrassbooks.com.

Printed in China.

18   17   16   15   14   1   2   3   4   5

All photos by Lynn Donaldson except for:

Pages 26, 27, 28, 110

Photography by Gib Myers

Acknowledgments

Dorothy and Gerald Glaser; Val Jacobson and Jena Finley; At Home on the Range; Gourmet Cellar; Montana Fish Company; Livingston Kite Company; Natural Resources Defense Council; World Wildlife Fund; American Prairie Reserve; Costco; MARS, Inc.; D'amico Catering; Depuy Spring Creek; Dale and Margaret Vermillion; Jen, Pat, Josie and Isla Vermillion; Sweetwater Travel; Les Berthy; Eric Paramore; Henry Harrison; Clyde Aspevig and Carol Guzman; Jim and Linda Harrison; Michael Keaton; Colin, Isabel and Simone Davis; Dan, Charlie, Ben and Chase Vermillion; Evie Cranston; Carl and Elizabeth Webb; Meredith Brokaw; Russell Chatham; Gem and Mark George; The Mary Grace Family; The Boreham Family; Malou Flato and John Taliaferro; Susan and Jeff Bridges; Diane Stillman and Elaine Uehlin; Lee Kinsey and Secluded Waters Outfitters; Gib and Susan Myers; the Hudson Family; Tumblewood Teas. And a special acknowledgement to Montana Party Rentals. Thank you to all of the supporters of our Kickstarter.com campaign, including Colin K. Davis, Deb Endres and Jean Heishman Grant.

406-222-8884 ~ www.MustangCatering.com

CONTENTS

FOREWORD

When Mike Art bought Chico Hot Springs in Montana, in the early 1970s, it was a derelict liability threatening to collapse. Not much was noticeably done to correct that until 1977. Realizing you could not expect to have a successful hotel, from the second story of which you could clearly see the exact geographic middle of nowhere, without a restaurant, he proceeded to build one.

A rustic dining room was constructed to suit the locale, but the menu was anything but rustic. I first set foot in it one evening on the way back from a fishing trip to Yellowstone Park with John Bailey. Fresh oysters? Duck? What the hell was going down here?

It turned out the chef, a seemingly callow youth named Larry Edwards, had been recruited up from Jackson Hole. Frankly, I don't recall that whole original menu, but baked brie and sole en croute were most assuredly not items one encountered at that time on menus anywhere west of Chicago or east of San Francisco.

A few years later, Edwards moved on, and while Chico was and remains a good place to eat years later, the brilliance he initially brought to the venue went with him. As the eighties became the nineties, many, including myself, literally begged him to open his own restaurant in Livingston, but for reasons known only to him it never happened.

Finally, by 1994, it was clear no one was going to step up to bat, and I began laying awake nights thinking about how I might do it. The only real estate that made sense was the Livingston Bar and Grille, which had been purchased by Mike Art, and over which Edwards presided for a few years. But then it was sold to people who had no business owning a restaurant and under whose tenure it degenerated into a filthy, mouse-infested ptomaine emporium.

Naturally, they put it up for sale, but at a price so absurd no one could buy it, as they would be hopelessly buried in debt from day one. In early 1995, I sat down with my friend and realtor Ernie Meador and tried to figure out the lowest offer the desperate owners would accept. All the serious buyers had come and gone, and no one had looked at it in two years. When we made our offer, they accepted it instantly like a trout inhaling a mayfly.

It took more than a few minutes for me to adjust to the fact I was now a restaurant owner. I had no culinary training. But what I did have was an abiding interest in fine cuisine aided and abetted by having eaten hundreds and hundreds of times in most of the best restaurants in America and quite a few in Europe as well. And I had watched and paid attention to how and why certain independently owned establishments flourished while others failed.

A year before the restaurant opened, I hand-selected the whole waitstaff from among the best servers I knew from various places in the region. My good friend Peter Lewis, then owner of Campagne, the best restaurant in Seattle, offered to come and formally train them in American Bistro service, which he did. But the kitchen remained a blank page.

I placed ads in the various papers, asking for resumés. The first one I got was from a girl named Carole Glaser in Minneapolis. It seemed her aunt who lived up on the Musselshell had seen the ad and forwarded it to her. She worked for the D'Amico Brothers, with whom I was familiar because of personal business meetings in the Twin Cities.

I liked Carole's credentials. She wanted to work and live in Montana after having visited Chico Hot Springs a few years earlier. So I popped three one hundred dollar bills into an envelope and asked her to head West. As she tells it today, her friends warned her something must be fishy. "Who sends someone they don't even know three hundred dollars in cash? You'd better be careful." Years later, Carole could reply, "Russell Chatham, that's who."

Then, there she was. As I recall, I hired her about five minutes into the interview. Clearly, she was beautiful, smart, vivacious and competent. Any unprofessional notions I may have otherwise had toward her were completely kept at bay by the fact that I was bulletproof in love with someone who had me on a short leash, which kept my eyes focused straight ahead.

The early years of the Bar and Grille, with respect to the kitchen, tended to be somewhat unpredictable. I was earning a Ph.D. in what-can-go-wrong-in-the-restaurant-business, but Carole was unflappable. And never once was I moved to regret my initial three hundred dollar investment. Still, I could sense she smelled the smoke of a distant fire. She wanted something of her own, and who could blame her? But it wasn't that she was running from a ship with a loose cannon or two. She wanted to be her own boss.

Not long after leaving my employ, she hung out a shingle upon which the lettering read, "Mustang Catering." Her space was rather outside the downtown business district, but that didn't matter. It wasn't strictly catering. She ran it as a lunch restaurant as well. In Livingston, as in all western towns at the time, good, clean, interesting cuisine was scarce. Sadly, most of the populace could not have cared less about fresh, thoughtfully prepared food, but enough did to keep Carole busy and thriving. Elizabeth and I ate there every day, grateful for someone who dared to defy the grim status quo.

Being rather deeply immersed in keeping my own place afloat, it took some time to register that Carole was keeping company with a handsome, and, thank God, decent young man. Before we knew it, wedding bells were ringing and Carole Glaser became Mrs. Dan Sullivan, and before we could even process that, they were three with a special little boy underfoot.

To keep a short story as short as possible—all the while, Carole was developing her catering business with a focus on quality. Eventually, people of taste began hiring her regularly to do their special events. They knew she could be counted on not to cut corners and to deliver as promised.

When I created the new Livingston Bar and Grille, my overriding intent was to build something uniquely beautiful and quality-oriented in a place which never had such a thing. The idea was to give the town something of which it could really be proud.

There were many facets in realizing and then maintaining such an enterprise, naturally, but perhaps the most important of these was having help who showed up regularly on time, then performed their jobs conscientiously and with pride. Chief among these was Carole.

Professional kitchen work is anything but glamorous in spite of how it might look through television's fantasy lens. It's a precise, slow-going business, often hot and unsung, and for which pancake makeup and a chef's coat with your giant initials on it are of no use.

What I admire about Carole Sullivan is her appropriate attitude toward, and commitment to, her chosen craft. As J. S. Bach famously said, "Be content with your fate, for that's the only road to happiness there is." Over these many years, I've watched Carole show up for work, her own restaurant now, seriously, but cheerfully, and with a guiding sense of humor. Through this she has gained well-earned credentials and wide respect, making in the process a good, dignified life for herself and her family, and that's everything.

– Russell Chatham

Introduction: The Mustang Story

Rushing around the Mustang kitchen, preparing food for the café and frantically checking off the tasks to get ready for one catering gig after another in the peak of summer, I am grateful—stressed, but grateful. My husband Dan and I have a successful business in a beautiful community. Our son, Henry, is growing up in and around the shop—he always knows where to find me! He worries that Mom works too hard.

Seventeen years ago I would never have imagined my life this way. It has been a good journey. Elements of my experience are in the food that I prepare. That's the way it is with cooking, but this book is also proof that there isn't a recipe for life.

During the years I have operated Mustang Fresh Food and Catering, the question I hear the most is, "Where did you learn how to cook?" It's funny, because as a young person, I never planned on this as a career. I never stood next to my mother while she cooked our family meals every night and dreamed of owning my own restaurant.

But I believe that everything happens for a reason—and this is what happened.

I grew up in North Dakota, but my career started in Minneapolis working in a record store. From there I went deeper into the music business, and for 11 years I worked for major record labels in several different capacities. It was an exciting time for a young girl in her 20s to fall into a job that let her meet and hang out with rock and roll legends like Tina Turner, Bob Seger, Huey Lewis, Pat Benatar, David Bowie and so many others. But after a while the scene got tiresome. When a good friend offered me an opportunity to open a coffee shop in a new business venture where she envisioned a music store that also sold books and coffee (long before Barnes & Noble), I took it. Did I know anything about running a coffee shop? Not a lick, but I did it anyway and learned as I went along.

What I learned is that just because a location is great for selling coffee, doesn't mean it's a good place to sell music. The place closed and we split ways.

But running my coffee shop gave me a whole new connection to the food industry; I gravitated toward it. I found that (much like the music business), restaurateurs and caterers are pretty much crazy, and I loved it. I ended up working for a fabulous restaurant company called D'amico Catering, run by amazing brothers who owned many restaurants throughout the Twin Cities. I learned so much at this job, I considered going to culinary school. My boss told me simply, "Why should you pay to go to school when you can get paid to learn everything you need to know working here?" That's what I did, gaining the fundamentals of cooking—sauces, stocks, ratios, flavors, volume, kitchen management—on the job. It was frenetic and wonderful.

But soon my spirit longed for something else. I felt the need to be connected with a smaller community. No more keeping up with the Joneses. A simpler life.

I spent a lot of time in Montana as a child. My mother's siblings all lived out here, and something told me that this is where I needed to be. So I packed up. My Australian Shepherd, Hannah, and I spent two weeks traveling throughout Montana, looking for the right fit. I stayed at Chico Hot Springs for a few days during a family reunion and enjoyed an afternoon in Livingston. Soon after that, my aunt told me about an artist named Russell Chatham who was planning to open a restaurant in Livingston.

This was it. I sent him a resumé and in short order, I got a response from the artist. He sent an envelope with three one hundred dollar bills and a handwritten note telling me to buy an airline ticket to interview for the position. I had no idea who Russell Chatham was at the time; I wondered what kind of person sends cash in the mail. I wasn't sure what I was getting into, but, of course, I took the job.

A month later I made my way to Livingston and got to know Russell. I found that his Impressionist landscape paintings captured the essence of Montana and his character reflected the quirky, sometimes wild, nature of Livingston. But the restaurant wasn't ready to open as planned. The staff was waiting in the wings. Within a week of my arrival, Russell fired the executive chef. The task of running the restaurant was left to the pastry chef and me, the only ones who knew what was going on in the kitchen. It was baptism by fire.

After about six months of running and gunning the kitchen at the Bar and Grille, I'd had enough. This wasn't what I'd expected. I realized that my real passion was catering.

I started small. My first gigs were at the Livingston Country Club handling food for golf tournaments (Ladies Day, Men's Night, etc.). In exchange, they let me use their kitchen for my own catering jobs. It was a great arrangement, and I met some wonderful people, most notably, my future husband, Dan Sullivan.

Through word of mouth, my business grew. Little by little, Dan began helping me more and more in the kitchen. It just seemed like the timing was right. So many well-traveled people were moving here and the demand increased for a caterer who would add a little extra something to their events.

Then the fabulous Jewel Redmon came into my life. We became friends through her daughter, Jill, who owned Montana Party Rentals. I catered Jill's wedding, and afterwards, Jewel gave me a proposal: If I would come and help with her events, I could use her kitchen and continue building my own business. Working with Jewel was magical. She was

the most pleasant, beautiful, hard-working woman I have ever had the chance to meet. She introduced me to groups in Yellowstone National Park, most memorably an organization whose members visit for a week each year to watch the wolves. They needed all their meals catered for the week, which meant a lot of early mornings, long afternoons and late nights, but it was a wonderful time. I loved working with Jewel, but I also had a vision of growing my catering business along with a small retail store.

Next, I went out on my own. Dan and I found a space for Mustang Catering at the far end of Main Street. At the same time, we found out I was pregnant. (When it rains, it pours.) We started out just catering that first summer, and while I was working on an order for a dinner party one afternoon, my water broke six weeks early.

I was rushed to the hospital and flown to Billings. There, we sat for five days, me trying to figure out how to cater two weddings and Dan trying to figure out how to support me. Henry was born on September 19, 2002, a little 4.9-pound wiffett. After three weeks in the neo-natal wing, we finally got back to Livingston and settled into family life. But it wasn't long before I had to get back into the kitchen.

Since then, Mustang has expanded and moved locations. Somehow people found us, and we started building a solid clientele, including regulars like Michael Keaton, Jeff Bridges and his family. I can still remember the very first phone messages from both of them and how excited I was that they actually wanted me to provide food for them. That was many years ago, but it's still a thrill to work with these longtime customers and all the others who've helped Mustang Fresh Food and Catering grow.

Through the years, what I've learned is there isn't always a recipe for life. I became a restaurant owner through a series of unexpected events; I gained my skills on the ground and running. More often than not I rely on simplicity: Keep it real. So,

I make honest food with fresh ingredients. I look at the framed pictures on the wall of the Mustang Café, artful illustrations of fruit and vegetables, and I see beautiful ingredients. That's how I think of my food: uncomplicated and delicious.

Despite the fact that I have had the honor of cooking for President Obama and Martha Stewart, it's the regular customers who come into the shop every day who make the effort worthwhile. My hope is that everything we offer at Mustang makes life simpler for our customers; I want to give people the opportunity to spend more time with their friends and families by preparing food that they love.

I don't know all of our customers by name—some I just know by what they order every time I see them in the shop. The pretty blonde who always gets Evil Jungle Chicken. The kids who come in for sweet treats after school. The teenager who loves the pulled pork sandwiches or the woman who cherry-picks all the chicken from the serve-yourself soup station.

Those are the regulars, and I don't know what we would do without them. But there are also customers who've become friends. These folks have their favorites, too. They have supported me through the years, and many of them have graciously allowed me to showcase their personal menus in the chapters of this book.

Whether it is a birthday party, a backyard barbecue or a holiday feast, I want to make meal-planning easier by putting these recipes together into "gatherings" so that you can create your own events with the people you love. With each recipe, I hope you feel like I'm right there in the kitchen alongside you, cooking these meals that have become favorites.

Carole Sullivan, Mustang proprietor

Dedications and Thank You

Dedicated to Dan and Henry.
My two best friends. Love you.

Many thanks to my editor Seabring Davis,
photographer Lynn Donaldson,
graphic design firm Engine 8,
and my friend Jill Redmon, without whom
this book would never have happened.
You believed in me when sometimes
I didn't believe in myself.

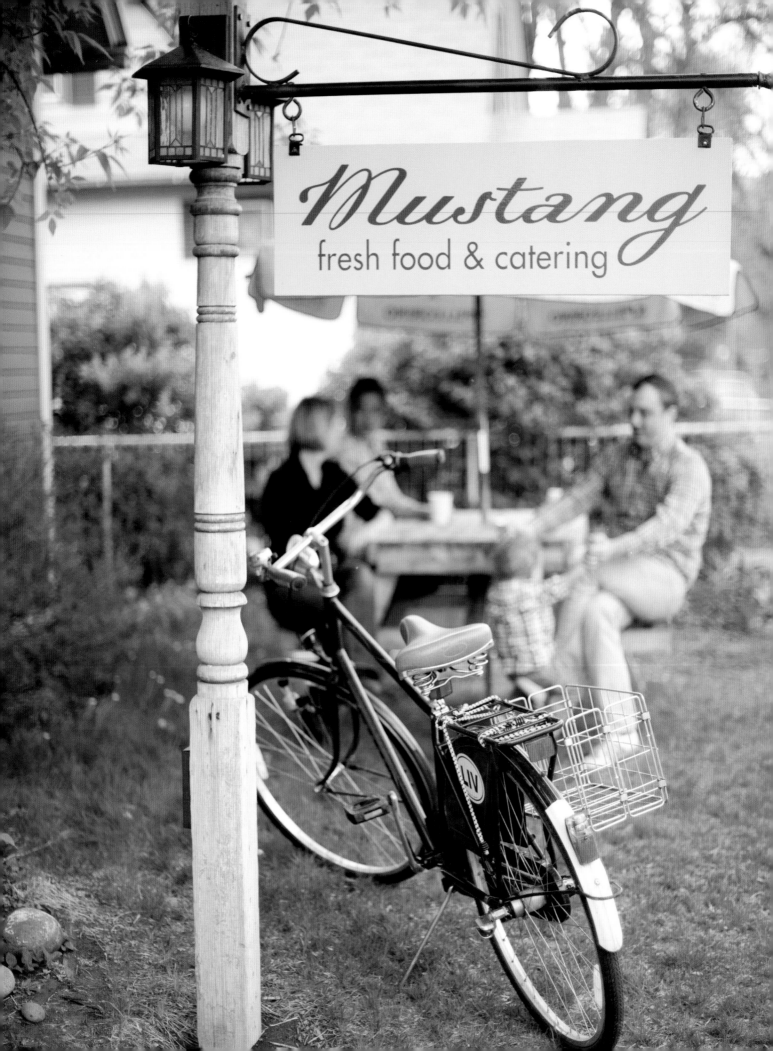

THE MUSTANG STANDARDS

Artichoke Parmesan Soup

Hearty Vegetable Soup

Indian Lamb Stew

Chicken Mirabella

Wild Mushroom Stroganoff

Pulled Pork Sandwich

Chicken Pot Pie

Lemon Blueberry Cupcakes

The Shop

The little red house on West Lewis Street in Livingston, Montana, is where it all happens. We've been in business since 1997, and this location is where I feel most at home. It's our shop and real kitchen, where customers come for meals they've grown to love. Here at the café, the fresh salad bar, hot bar, sandwich menu and daily soup offerings are what people have come to count on. I love being the place where they know the food is fresh, consistent and delicious.

Whether it's a business lunch, an after-school snack for the kids, a convenient weeknight meal or a pick-up for a party, it's here at Mustang. On any given day, these are the standard items available at the shop, for here or to go.

Ignatius Bunkers peers at the dessert choices at Mustang. Mini pot pies in-progress. Courtney Lehman takes a break for lunch. A great place to bring the kids (and canine friends, too) for a snack. Indian Lamb Stew.

• • • • Pulled Pork Sandwich. The daily salad bar accoutrements are fresh and varied. A busy day at the counter, where soups, sandwiches, salad bar and housemade favorites are available daily. Even cowboys like Mustang to-go!

ARTICHOKE PARMESAN SOUP

SERVES 6–8

- 2 tablespoons butter
- 4 Leeks sliced white part only, washed and drained
- 4 cups artichoke hearts packed in water
- 5 cups of chicken or vegetable stock
- ½ cup finely shredded Parmesan cheese
- 1 cup heavy cream
- salt and pepper to taste

1. Melt butter over medium heat. Add leeks, cooking and stirring until leeks are softened—about 10 minutes. Add artichoke hearts and stock. Bring soup to a simmer and let cook for about 20 minutes.

2. Purée soup in batches, using a small ladle to push soup through fine mesh strainer. This will catch all the unwanted artichoke pieces and give you a smooth consistency.

3. Stir in Parmesan, heavy cream and salt and pepper. Reheat soup to desired temperature.

HEARTY VEGETABLE SOUP

SERVES 6–8

- 3 tablespoons Canola oil
- ½ cup each peeled and diced potato, yellow onion, carrot and celery
- 1 tablespoon chopped garlic
- 4 cups vegetable stock
- 1½ cups shredded cabbage
- 1 (14.5 ounce) can diced tomatoes
- 1 teaspoon dried Italian seasoning
- 1 bay leaf
- ½ cup frozen peas
- ½ cup frozen corn
- 2 tablespoons chopped flat leaf parsley
- 1 tablespoon chiffonade basil
- 1 tablespoon finely chopped fresh thyme
- ½ teaspoon salt
- ¼ teaspoon pepper

1. Heat oil over medium-high heat in stock pot. Sauté potatoes, onion, carrot, celery and garlic for about 5–6 minutes or until onions are soft, stirring frequently so vegetables won't stick to bottom of pan.

2. Add stock, cabbage and tomatoes along with dried Italian seasonings and bay leaf. Reduce heat to low and simmer for about 20 minutes or until potatoes are fork tender.

3. Stir in peas and corn and simmer 2 minutes longer. Add fresh herbs and salt and pepper.

INDIAN LAMB STEW

SERVES 8–10

7 tablespoons Canola oil

1 large onion, diced

1 tablespoon pickled jalapeño, diced

1 tablespoon garlic, chopped

2 lbs. lamb stew meat, cut into bit-size

2 cups diced tomatoes with juice (canned)

1 tablespoon cumin

2 teaspoons coriander

½ teaspoon turmeric

¼ teaspoon cayenne

2 teaspoons salt

1 lb. potatoes, peeled and cut into chunks

3⅔ cups water

1 cup frozen peas

1. Heat oil in heavy pot over medium-high heat. When hot, put in the onions, garlic and jalapeños. Stir and fry until the onions have browned slightly. Add the meat and stir vigorously for about 10–15 minutes, until meat is browned. Add the spices, stir to coat. Add tomatoes and continue to stir, cooking on high heat for 10–15 minutes or until the sauce is thick and the oil seems to separate from it.

2. Add water, cook for another 5 minutes, then add potatoes. Cover and leave the lid just slightly ajar. Adjust heat to medium-low and cook about 20–25 minutes or until the meat is tender and the sauce is thick.

3. Just before serving, stir in frozen peas, stir and cook for 1 minute. Serve warm over rice if desired.

CHICKEN MIRABELLA

SERVES 10–12

20 chicken thighs

3 tablespoons garlic, chopped

3 bay leaves

1 teaspoon dried oregano

1 cup red wine vinegar

1 cup olive oil

1 cup dried plums cut in half

1 cup green olives cut in thirds

¼ cup capers with some juice

1 cup brown sugar

1 cup white wine

1. Combine garlic, bay leaves, oregano, red wine vinegar, olive oil, dried plums, green olives and capers with some juice in a large container. Marinate the chicken thighs overnight.

2. Preheat oven to 350 degrees.

3. Pour brown sugar and white wine over chicken and bake uncovered for approximately 1 hour or until browned and cooked through.

4. Serve with warm couscous and dried currants and apricots.

WILD MUSHROOM STROGANOFF

SERVES 6–8

½ cup salted butter

¼ cup shallots, diced

5 lbs. wild mushrooms, cleaned, trimmed and sliced

1 cup cooking sherry

¾ cup vegetable stock

1 cup heavy cream

½ cup sour cream

⅓ cup Dijon mustard

sprinkle of salt and pepper

2 tablespoons fresh tarragon, chopped

1 tablespoon fresh dill, chopped

1. Melt butter in a large pan. Add shallots to the pan and cook for approximately 1 minute. Add wild mushrooms, cook for about 20–30 minutes, stirring occasionally until mushrooms are soft. Then add sherry and vegetable stock, cook down for 5 minutes.

2. Gently stir in heavy cream, sour cream and Dijon mustard. Season lightly with salt and pepper to taste. Let this simmer for 10 minutes, then add tarragon and dill.

3. Serve over egg noodles or brown rice.

PULLED PORK SANDWICH

SERVES 6–8

2 tablespoons ground cumin, curry powder and chili powder

1 tablespoon each ground allspice and black pepper

1 teaspoon ground cinnamon

4 lbs. of country style boneless pork ribs (available at your local butcher or Costco)

½ cup dry spice rub (see recipe)

¾ teaspoon kosher salt

¾ cup Sweet Baby Ray's BBQ Sauce (yes, there it is, my secret is out!)

SPICE RUB

1. Mix all ingredients together.

PULLED PORK

1. Rub dry spices into pork on all sides. Cover and let sit overnight in the refrigerator.

2. The next day, preheat oven 350 degrees. Generously season ribs with kosher salt, cover pan tightly with tin foil and bake for 2 to 2½ hours or until ribs are fork tender.

3. Remove from oven and let stand, covered. Be sure to keep the delicious pan juices. When the meat is cool enough to handle, shred into bite size chunks (I don't like to shred it too fine) in the same pan it was cooked.

4. Cover ribs with Famous Ray's BBQ Sauce (OK, the jig is up, but it is so good!). Mix together and reheat covered for 10–15 minutes at 350 degrees. Serve with our Classic Coleslaw (see recipe, page 50) on ciabatta bread.

CHICKEN POT PIE

SERVES 6–8

1 Torte Dough (or frozen puff pastry) (See recipe page 74)

½ cup butter

½ cup flour

4 cups chicken stock

1 teaspoon dried thyme

1 teaspoon kosher salt

½ teaspoon fresh ground pepper

3 cups roasted Costco chicken, shredded

1½ cups parboiled diced carrots

1 cup frozen peas

12 frozen pearl onions

1 whole egg

2 tablespoons milk or water

1. Lightly butter a 9x13-inch pan.

2. Cut chilled dough in half. You will use only one half for this recipe; wrap the other half in plastic and freeze for up to 2 months. Divide remaining dough in half and roll out one for bottom layer of the pan and the other for top of torte. Use flour on both sides while rolling out as to not stick to the surface.

3. Begin to make a roux by melting butter. After it has melted whisk in flour. After flour is incorporated (about 1 minute) slowly add chicken stock whisking constantly as you are adding. Add thyme, salt and pepper and stir.

4. After all chicken stock has been incorporated and you have a silky sauce, add the chicken, carrots, peas and pearl onions.

5. Allow to cool, then spoon into prepared dough pan. Roll out dough to cover and slightly overhang the pie pan, trimming some of the ends and then rolling dough to seal by crimping the dough.

6. Make 3–4 slits into top of pie dough to allow steam to vent. Make an egg wash by mixing the egg and water or milk, then brush the pastry with it.

8. Preheat oven to 400 degrees. Bake for 13 minutes and then reduce oven to 350 degrees and continue to bake for about another 35 minutes or until the crust is nice and brown and you can see the sauce is bubbling. Serve with a green salad and enjoy.

LEMON BLUEBERRY CUPCAKES
MAKES 24 CUPCAKES

3¼ cups all-purpose flour

1¼ cup sugar

1 tablespoon baking powder

½ teaspoon kosher salt

¼ teaspoon baking soda

6 tablespoons unsalted butter, melted

¼ cup Canola oil

2 large eggs

1 cup buttermilk

1 cup whole milk

1 teaspoon vanilla extract

1 teaspoon lemon zest

1¼ cup frozen blueberries

2¼ cups sifted powder sugar

10 tablespoons unsalted butter, room temperature

½ cup Xylitol (this is a natural sugar substitute that is more granular than regular sugar)

½ teaspoon kosher salt

1¼ teaspoon vanilla extract

1 teaspoon grated lemon peel

4 teaspoons whole milk

blueberries, for garnish

CUPCAKES

1. Preheat oven to 350 degrees. Spray two 12 cup muffin pans with cooking spray and line with paper liners. Sift flour and next four ingredients into a large bowl. Whisk melted butter and oil in medium bowl. Add eggs, whisk until blended. Whisk buttermilk, milk, vanilla extract and lemon zest. Add buttermilk mixture to dry ingredients, whisk just to blend. Stir in frozen blueberries. Divide batter among liners. (I use a commercial-size 1⅝-ounce scoop).

2. Bake cupcakes until tester inserted into center comes out clean, about 23 minutes. Transfer cupcakes to rack to cool.

FROSTING

1. Combine first 6 ingredients in the bowl of an electric mixer. Add 4 teaspoons milk. Beat until well blended and fluffy, adding more milk by the teaspoon if dry, about 4 minutes total.

2. When cupcakes are cool, pipe frosting onto cupcakes with a 12-inch bag pastry bag using a round tip.

3. Place 5 fresh blueberries on each cupcake.

THE WILDERNESS BRUNCH

Menu

Whole Chilled Salmon
with Cucumber Dill Sauce

Orzo Salad

French Potato Salad

Minted Pea Soup

Huckleberry-Peach Crisp

Natural Resources Defense Council

Longtime advocates and protectors of wildlife, Natural Resources Defense Council holds its annual donor tour in Yellowstone National Park every May. I've had the honor of being a part of it for several years.

It's become a tradition to have the Whole Chilled Salmon dinner at the Yellowstone picnic area near Lamar Valley after a day of watching bears, bison, big horn sheep and hopefully wolves.

As everyone here in Montana knows, the weather is always changing, and as hardy as this group was, the evening became very cool and the skies started drizzling. After grazing on appetizers and soup, we headed back to our digs at the rustic Range Rider Inn in Silvergate for a meal that is as beautiful as it is yummy.

· · · · Fresh Orzo Salad. The Mustang Catering van delivers. Huckleberry-Peach Crisp. Minted Pea Soup. A walk in the wilderness.

· · · · A well-fed raven in Yellowstone National Park. French Potato Salad.
A guest serves Whole Chilled Salmon. Artisan cheese plate in the wild.
One happy customer Gib Myers enjoys an après-hike glass of wine.

WHOLE CHILLED SALMON

SERVES 10–12

1 (4 to 5 lb.) side of wild salmon, skin on

8 cups Court Bouillon (recipe follows)

1 large English cucumber

Note: Photo to the left depicts a whole salmon.

1. This recipe is best prepared a day ahead of serving.

2. Preheat oven to 375 degrees.

3. Pour Court Bouillon onto prepared 22 x 16-inch sheet pan. Place 20 x 14-inch cookie drying rack on top of the sheet pan and spray rack with cooking spray, so fish won't stick. Place fish skin side down on rack. Spray a piece of tin foil with cooking spray and place over fish wrapping around sheet pan to trap steam. Place fish with the rack into the oven and cook for approximately 25–30 minutes or until thickest part of salmon springs back slightly to your touch.

4. Carefully remove pan from oven and allow to sit for 20 minutes. Remove fish with cookie drying rack onto a clean sheet pan and cool in the refrigerator overnight or at least 2 hours.

5. Decorate fish with thinly sliced cucumber rounds. Serve with Cucumber Dill Sauce (see recipe, page 32).

COURT BOUILLON

MAKES 8½ CUPS

8 cups of fish stock or chicken stock

1 bay leaf

2 whole cloves

2 sprigs each fresh thyme and parsley

1 teaspoon whole peppercorns

1½ teaspoon kosher salt

¼ cup red wine vinegar

¼ cup white wine

¾ cup carrot, diced

¾ cup celery, diced

¾ cup yellow onion, diced

1. Place all ingredients in a large stock pot.

2. Over high heat, bring to a boil. Let simmer for about 10 minutes, skimming off any residue that builds up.

3. Strain ingredients over a bowl, pressing down with a ladle to extract all of the flavors.

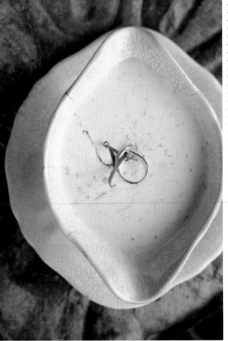

Cucumber Dill Sauce

MAKES 2 ½ CUPS

1 cup of mayonnaise

½ cup of yogurt

¼ cup of sour cream

6 cornichons, finely diced

¾ cup English cucumber, diced

1 tablespoon fresh dill, chopped

1 tablespoon fresh flat leaf parsley, chopped

1 tablespoon shallot, finely diced

1 tablespoon Dijon mustard

1 tablespoon lemon juice

1 dash of Tabasco

1. Put all ingredients in the bowl of a food processor and pulse 3 or 4 times until ingredients are combined.

2. Refrigerate until ready to serve.

Orzo Salad

SERVES 8–10

1 lb. of cooked orzo (follow instructions on package)

¼ cup olive oil

¾ cup crumbled feta cheese

¾ cup chopped canned roasted red peppers, rinsed and drained

¾ cup frozen peas, thawed

¼ cup fresh mint, chopped and packed

¼ cup toasted pine nuts

salt and pepper to taste

1. Cook orzo according to instructions on package.

2. After orzo has cooled, add the rest of the ingredients and toss gently.

FRENCH POTATO SALAD

SERVES 8–10

- 10 small- to medium-sized Yukon Gold potatoes
- 1½ teaspoons kosher salt
- ½ cup Dijon shallot vinaigrette (See recipe page 83)
- 2 tablespoons capers
- 1½ teaspoons fresh tarragon, chopped
- salt and pepper to taste

1. Peel potatoes and slice thin, about ⅛-inch thick on a mandolin (or by hand). Place in a stock pot, cover potatoes with water and cook over a high flame. Add salt. As soon as water begins to boil, turn the heat down to medium so you have a rolling boil. Let potatoes cook for about 5 minutes or until fork tender.

2. Drain potatoes in a colander and cool.

3. Once cooled, toss with the rest of the ingredients.

MINTED PEA SOUP

SERVES 6–8

- 2 tablespoons butter
- 1½ cup onion, chopped
- 6 cups frozen sweet baby peas
- 6 cups chicken or vegetable stock
- ⅓ cup mint leaves (packed)
- ¼ cup heavy cream (optional)

1. Melt butter over low to medium heat. Add onions, cooking and stirring until onions are softened, about 10 minutes.

2. When onions are softened, add frozen peas, stir to coat about 1 minute and add stock. Turn heat up a little and bring to a boil. Add mint leaves and turn down, simmering soup for about 15 minutes.

3. Purée soup in batches.

4. Using a small ladle, push soup through a fine mesh strainer to give your soup a fine consistency.

5. Stir in optional heavy cream and season to taste with salt and pepper. Reheat soup before serving.

HUCKLEBERRY-PEACH CRISP

SERVES 10–12

- 1 cup brown sugar
- 1 cup quick oats
- 1½ cups flour
- 1 cup chilled butter, diced

- 2 cups fresh or frozen huckleberries
- 2 cups fresh peaches, skins and pits removed, sliced (try white peaches if they are available)
- ½ – ¾ cup sugar depending on sweetness of fruit
- 3 tablespoons flour
- 2 tablespoons ground nutmeg
- ½ teaspoon ground cinnamon

TOPPING

1. Thoroughly mix together by hand or in mixer.

FILLING

1. Preheat oven to 375 degrees.

2. Mix together gently to combine ingredients. Spoon into a 9x12 inch baking dish and finish with topping.

3. Bake for 20 to 25 minutes until topping is golden brown. This works with most fruits if you can't find huckleberries or if peaches are out of season.

Kitchen Dish

Jarred spices such as nutmeg and cinnamon lose their freshness quickly. Stores that carry spices in bulk are your best bet. Buy only what you need so that your spices stay fresh for more flavorful dishes.

AL FRESCO ON THE RANGE

Menu

Bison Short Ribs Provençal

Creamy Polenta

French Green Beans

Balsamic Vinaigrette
with Mixed Greens

Catfish Fingers
with Lemon Tarragon Sauce

Lemon-Goat Cheese Cheesecake

I am willing to travel five hours away for this client's event, including hours on a dirt road with no cell phone service while passing only a few farms and antelope along the way. Once I get there, it's always worth the trip.

In creating a large prairie-based reserve for wildlife and the public, APR has connected with MARS, Inc., the American global manufacturer of confectionery, and the MARS Ambassador Program, which focuses on corporate responsibility by promoting employee volunteerism. This group, from all over the world, helped to build trails and remove structures that block animal movement. Hard work should be rewarded with good food, so the group enjoyed a dinner with Catfish Fingers as a starter and a main course of Bison Short Ribs that has become a favorite up on the prairie — a Montana "surf & turf."

Yurt camp on the American Prairie Reserve. Montana mule, a refreshing cocktail. Campfire tales. A MARS, Inc. ambassador traveled thousands of miles just for a Mustang meal.

Roughing it. Catfish Fingers and Lemon Tarragon Sauce. Drizzling Balsamic Vinaigrette on mixed greens. Bison Short Ribs Provençal with Creamy Polenta and French Green Beans. Dining on the prairie.

BISON SHORT RIBS PROVENÇAL

SERVES 8–10

5 to 6 lbs. of bison short ribs (approximately 10 ribs)

(Beef short ribs can be used as a substitute, of course.)

2 tablespoons olive oil

1½ cups red wine

2 cups beef broth

½ cup yellow onions, diced

½ cup medium carrots, peeled and diced

½ cup celery, diced

1 tablespoon garlic, chopped

2 cups canned diced tomatoes

1 bay leaf

2 fresh thyme sprigs

2 fresh parsley sprigs

1 cup Kalamata olives, sliced

1 tablespoon lemon zest

¼ cup flat leaf parsley, chopped

¼ cup fresh thyme, chopped

1. Salt and pepper ribs. In a large oven-safe pot, on medium-high heat, brown ribs in olive oil on both sides, about 8 minutes. This needs to be done in two batches. Once browned, use tongs to remove ribs and set aside.

2. In the same pot that was used to brown ribs, add red wine and scrape up brown bits collected from ribs on bottom of pan.

3. Add beef broth to wine and stir for another minute. Next add all of the vegetables, including the canned tomatoes, garlic and bay leaf. Bring to a boil for about 5 minutes.

4. Preheat oven to 325 degrees.

5. Add ribs and fresh herbs to the boiling liquid. Cover the pot with foil and place in the preheated oven.

6. Bake for 2½ hours and occasionally change the position of the ribs for optimum cooking. It's ready when the meat is falling-off-the-bone tender.

7. Ideally, you'll need a large over-safe pot or roasting pan with a lid. If you don't have one, before baking, transfer ribs to a large baking dish and cover tightly with foil.

8. Top with Kalamata olives and lemon zest, then garnish with flat leaf parsley and fresh thyme.

9. Serve over Creamy Polenta (recipe follows).

CREAMY POLENTA

SERVES 8–10

- 2 cups of polenta
- 8 cups of chicken stock
- 4 tablespoons unsalted butter
- ½ teaspoon salt
- ¼ teaspoon pepper
- ¼ cup Parmesan cheese (optional)

1. Bring stock to a boil in a stock pot.

2. Slowly whisk in polenta. Whisk constantly for about 2–3 minutes.

3. Turn burner to low and stir every few minutes with a wooden spoon so polenta won't stick to bottom of pan.

4. After about 15 minutes, add butter, salt, pepper and optional Parmesan cheese.

FRENCH GREEN BEANS

SERVES 8–10

- 2 lbs. of French green beans
- 1 tablespoon salt
- ⅓ cup blood orange avocado oil (available at Gourmet Cellar or specialty shops)
- 1 rounded tablespoon coarse sea flakes (available at Gourmet Cellar or specialty shops)
- ¾ teaspoon ground pepper

1. Bring 16 cups of water to a boil in a large stock pot.

2. Add salt and French green beans. Over a rolling boil, cook beans for about 8 minutes, or until al dente.

3. Immediately drain beans in a colander.

4. Once drained, place beans in a large bowl filled with ice water. Allow to cool for about 10 minutes. Drain beans again.

5. Place beans in a bowl with oil, salt and pepper and toss to coat. Reheat beans in a casserole pan uncovered in a 350-degree oven for about 8–10 minutes or serve cold as a salad.

BALSAMIC VINAIGRETTE WITH MIXED GREENS

MAKES 3 CUPS

½ cup Dijon mustard

½ cup balsamic vinegar

2 cups olive oil

1. Whisk Dijon mustard and vinegar together in a bowl, then slowly whisk in olive oil.

2. Toss with greens and serve.

CATFISH FINGERS WITH LEMON TARRAGON SAUCE

SERVES 8–10

1 shallot, finely diced

2 tablespoons fresh tarragon, chopped

Juice of 1½ lemons

2 cups mayonnaise (Hellmann's or Best Foods)

salt and pepper to taste

6 (4–5 ounce) pieces of catfish

1 cup buttermilk

2 eggs

2 dashes of Tabasco

1 cup flour

1 teaspoon salt

½ teaspoon black pepper

4 cups toasted bread crumbs or Panko

1½ to 2 cups Canola oil

LEMON TARRAGON

1. Mix all ingredients together thoroughly.

2. Refrigerate until ready to serve.

CATFISH FINGERS

1. Cut catfish into 2-inch-wide by 4-inch-long strips.

2. In a bowl, whisk together buttermilk, eggs and Tabasco. In a separate bowl, mix flour, salt and pepper. In a third bowl, place breadcrumbs.

3. Dredge fish in flour, shaking off excess, then dip in buttermilk mixture, and then coat in bread crumbs.

4. Prepare a platter by placing paper towels over the top to drain the fish after frying.

5. Heat oil in a 12-inch frying pan over medium-high heat, until almost smoking.

6. Fry fish fingers 6 to 7 minutes per side, or until golden brown. Remove each from pan and drain on paper-towel-covered platter.

7. Serve warm with Lemon Tarragon Sauce.

LEMON-GOAT CHEESE CHEESECAKE

MAKES ONE 9-INCH CHEESECAKE

⅔ cup butter, at room temperature

½ cup confectioner's sugar

1½ cups, plus 2 tablespoons sifted all-purpose flour

½ teaspoon salt

SHORTBREAD CRUST

1. Preheat oven to 350 degrees.

2. In the bowl of an electric mixer on medium speed, cream the butter. Then add the sugar gradually and beat until fluffy.

3. Sift flour and salt into the creamed mixture and blend thoroughly. Bring the dough together into a ball with your hands and then flatten into a disc onto a floured surface.

4. Press the mixture evenly into the bottom of a parchment-lined springform pan. Bake the crust for 20 minutes or until golden brown. Allow the crust to cool completely.

2 lbs. cream cheese, room temperature

1 cup goat cheese (chevre), room temperature

1¼ cups sugar

2 eggs

3 teaspoons lemon zest

4 tablespoons fresh squeezed lemon juice

CHEESECAKE

1. Preheat oven to 350 degrees.

2. Using an electric mixer, beat the cream cheese until light and smooth. Add the goat cheese and sugar, continue to beat on medium speed. Add the eggs one at a time.

3. Blend in the lemon zest and juice. Pour mixture into the cooled crust.

4. Set the cheesecake into a roasting pan and add enough water to the pan to reach halfway up the sides of the cheesecake pan.

5. Bake in the oven for approximately 1 hour or until the cake is set and the top is golden brown.

6. Remove the cake from the roasting pan and place on a wire rack. Allow cake to cool slightly, then place the cake in the refrigerator for 6 hours or overnight.

BARBECUE ON THE RANCH

Menu

Stuffed Jalapeños

Classic Coleslaw

Calico Beans

Cowboy Stuffed Potatoes

Mixed Grill with Herb Oil

Sweet & Salty Pecan Bars

Huckleberry Bars

Elizabeth and Carl Webb

It's possible that I've cooked more dinners at West Creek Ranch than anywhere else. I started doing small dinners for Carl and Elizabeth in 1998. I think it was painter Russell Chatham who gave them my name for a small event with friends, and ever since then we've had a close relationship. I've watched West Creek Ranch grow not only in the number of beautiful buildings they've added, but also in the number of family members. I wasn't at Carl and Elizabeth's very intimate wedding, but I was never so happy to see two people tie the knot.

Their branding is a staple that I have now catered for 12 years. Of course, I don't do all of the cooking. I leave the meat to the real experts. In this chapter, I have included their son Brice Webb's famous Stuffed Jalapeños.

• • • • Each spring, good neighbors pitch in to help round-up cattle and share a fine meal after a hard day's work. Chicken on the grill. Classic Coleslaw. Elizabeth Webb, branding calves.

Aubrey eyes the dessert first! A cowboy works the herd.
A full plate with all the fixings. Brice and Jay, the grillmen.

STUFFED JALAPEÑOS
SERVES 12

- 24 large jalapeños, topped and seeds removed
- ½ lb. breakfast sausage
- 8 ounces cream cheese
- 1 tablespoon salt
- 1 tablespoon Cajun seasoning (favorite: Tony Chacheres)
- 1 lb. bacon, cut into 24 2-inch strips

1. In a sauce pan brown breakfast sausage. When cooked, remove and chop very fine. Return to the pan and add cream cheese, salt and Cajun seasoning. Mix thoroughly.

2. To fill peppers, place mixture in a pastry bag or Ziploc bag. If using a plastic bag, cut a small hole in the corner and squeeze mixture into peppers. Finish by topping peppers with bacon, securing with a toothpick.

3. Grill over mesquite coals, medium heat for 30–45 minutes. As the peppers cook they drip large quantities of oil, which reduces their spice level. Be careful with the oil dripping onto your fire; it can cause a flare up and burn the bottom of your peppers! Peppers can also be cooked in the oven at 300 degrees for the same amount of time, or until soft.

CLASSIC COLESLAW
SERVES 10–12

- 8 cups cabbage, shredded
- 2 cups carrot, peeled and shredded
- 1½ cups Broccoli Dressing (See recipe on page 85)
- ½ cup buttermilk
- 2 tablespoons Dijon mustard
- 1 teaspoon celery seed
- 3-4 shakes Tabasco
- salt and pepper to taste

1. Toss all ingredients in a large bowl until thoroughly combined.

2. Combine 1½ cups of Broccoli Dressing with slaw mixture until completely coated. You may need to add more so that coleslaw is liberally dressed.

3. Salt and pepper to taste.

CALICO BEANS

SERVES 10–12

3 (16.5-ounce) cans Bush's Baked Beans

1 (15-ounce) can ranch style beans

1 (15-ounce) can black beans, rinsed and drained

1 (15-ounce) can lima beans, rinsed and drained

1 (15-ounce can) white beans, rinsed and drained

2 tablespoons, plus 2 teaspoons Dijon mustard

2 tablespoons apple cider vinegar

2 tablespoons molasses

2 tablespoons, plus 2 teaspoons caramelized onions, chopped

2 tablespoons, plus 2 teaspoons cooked bacon, chopped

¼ cup brown sugar

3 dashes of Tabasco

¾ cup ketchup

1 tablespoon Worcestershire sauce

1. Preheat oven to 350 degrees.

2. Place all ingredients in a Dutch oven or other casserole dish. Stir to mix.

3. Bake in oven for 25–30 minutes or until beans are browned and bubbly.

COWBOY STUFFED POTATOES

SERVES 8

4 large Russet potatoes (¾ lb. each)

1 teaspoon salt

½ teaspoon pepper

2 tablespoons olive oil

2 tablespoons heavy cream

2 tablespoons butter, melted

¼ cup sour cream

4 green onions, sliced

½ teaspoon salt

¼ teaspoon pepper

For garnish

¼ cup bacon bits

½ cup cheddar cheese, shredded

⅓ cup sour cream

⅓ cup sliced green onions

1. Wash and dry potatoes. Rub with salt, pepper and olive oil. Place on a baking sheet pan in a 375-degree oven for 45 minutes or until potatoes are fork tender.

2. Allow potatoes to cool. When cool enough to handle, cut potatoes in half lengthwise. Scoop out flesh with a spoon, leaving enough of flesh in potato to keep its shape for stuffing later.

3. Mix potato flesh in a bowl with one tablespoon butter, sour cream, green onions, salt and pepper.

4. Stuff potato skins with mixture and brush the tops of potatoes with another tablespoon of melted butter. Place on sheet pan and broil for 10 minutes, or until nicely browned.

5. To serve, garnish with chopped bacon bits, shredded cheese, sour cream and sliced green onions.

Kitchen Dish

Heat your milk or cream before adding it to your favorite soup or warm dish to avoid curdling.

MIXED GRILL WITH HERB OIL

SERVES 10–12

- 2 tablespoons fresh thyme, chopped
- 2 cups basil leaves
- 1 cup flat leaf parsley, chopped
- 3 tablespoons garlic, chopped
- 1½ cups olive oil

HERB OIL

MAKES 2 CUPS

1. This is a all-purpose marinade that is perfect for meat, fish or vegetables. It's simple, delicious and versatile.

2. Place fresh herbs in a bowl of a food processor.

3. Blend until combined, about 10–15 seconds.

4. Slowly add olive oil until infused with the herbs.

- 2 lbs. chicken, fish or meat
- 1½ tablespoons herb oil
- salt and pepper to taste

GRILL

1. Heat an outdoor grill to medium-high heat.

2. Combine your choice of meat with herb oil, salt and pepper. Toss to coat completely. Let marinate for 10–15 minutes.

3. Depending on thickness and type of product, grill 6–10 minutes per side until cooked (fish will take less time).

4. For chicken breasts, cook 8 minutes per side.

Kitchen Dish

To retain moisture and avoid overcooking, mark your beef, pork and chicken on the grill in advance. Then just before serving, finish meat in a 350-degree oven, bringing it to the desired internal temperature.

Sweet & Salty Pecan Bars

MAKES 12

- ⅔ cup powdered sugar
- 2 cups all-purpose flour
- ¾ teaspoon salt
- 1 cup unsalted butter, softened

Crust

1. Preheat oven to 350 degrees.

2. Sift the powdered sugar, flour and salt together in a medium-sized bowl.

3. Beat the butter until creamy using a stand mixer fitted with a paddle attachment. Add the flour-sugar mixture to the butter and mix on low speed until fine crumbs form.

4. Gather the dough into a ball and press it into a 9x13-inch pan, distributing it as evenly as possible.

3. Bake for about 15 minutes until it starts to look dry but not browned. Let cool for 10–15 minutes.

- 10 tablespoons unsalted butter, melted
- ½ cup honey
- 3 tablespoons heavy cream
- ½ cup packed brown sugar
- ½ teaspoon salt
- 4 cups chopped pecans

Filling

1. Mix the melted butter, honey, cream, brown sugar and salt together in a medium sized bowl. Stir in the pecans and then spread the topping over the prepared crust.

2. Bake for about 25 minutes until set and golden brown. Let cool completely and then cut into squares.

Huckleberry Bars

MAKES 12

- ¾ cup unsalted butter, softened
- 1 cup light brown sugar
- 1½ cup all-purpose flour
- 1 teaspoon salt
- ½ teaspoon baking soda
- 1½ cups quick-cooking oatmeal
- 1¼ cups huckleberry jam

1. Preheat oven to 400 degrees.

2. For the crust, cream butter and sugar well in bowl of an electric mixer.

3. In a separate bowl, combine flour, salt and baking soda.

4. Stir into creamed mixture. When incorporated, stir in quick oatmeal, but don't over mix.

5. Press ¾ of the crust mixture into the bottom of a parchment-paper-lined 9x13-inch pan. Spread the jam on top and cover with the remaining crust mixture.

6. Bake about 12–15 minutes until light brown.

PATRIOTIC PARTY

Menu

Chicken Enchiladas

Turkey Chile Verde

Chile Rellenos Casserole

Grilled Vegetables

New Three Bean Salad

Summer Berry Pies

Michael Keaton

After years of catering actor Michael Keaton's Fourth of July party, I have to confess that it is still a thrill to get a call from Michael. At his Montana home on the Boulder River, this annual gathering is an easy affair where family and longtime friends ramble down the country road to visit, far away from the hubbub of town. It's Michael's comfortable nature and gracious hospitality that brings people together.

After all these years, Michael still requests the Turkey Chile Verde and other Mustang favorites. While some people would consider this menu "untraditional," it has certainly become a tradition at the Keaton Ranch.

· · · · Guest Thomas McGuane joins the annual July 4th backyard BBQ at Michael Keaton's house. A platter of Grilled Vegetables. Chicken Enchiladas. New Three Bean Salad. A quaint beverage table.

Charlie Kirn digs in. Turkey Chile Verde. Glamor girls. Pie in the Big Sky.
All smiles for a perfect summer day.

CHICKEN ENCHILADAS

SERVES 8

3 tablespoons Canola oil

1¼ cup onion, finely diced

1 tablespoon garlic, chopped

2½ tablespoons chili powder

1 tablespoon ground cumin

1 tablespoon ground coriander

pinch of cayenne

1 tablespoon sugar

2 teaspoons salt

1 teaspoon pepper

2 (13-ounce) cans of tomato sauce

1 roasted chicken, white and dark meat, shredded (I prefer the Costco chicken)

1½ cups water

½ cup cilantro, chopped

2 tablespoons pickled jalapeños, chopped

2 cups shredded pepper Jack and Cheddar cheese combined

1 cup shredded pepper Jack and Cheddar cheese combined for garnish

16 small corn tortillas

1. Pour oil in a deep sauce pan, after oil is hot add onions. Stir until soft, over low to medium flame 8–10 minutes.

2. Add chopped garlic and stir another minute or so.

3. Add the rest of your dry ingredients, stir for one minute.

4. Add tomato sauce and cook for another 10 minutes with dry ingredients.

5. Add chicken and 1 cup of water, simmer for 15–20 more minutes.

6. Pour mixture through a medium mesh strainer to extract liquid. This is the enchilada sauce.

7. Transfer chicken mixture to a bowl to cool, then add cilantro, jalapeños and cheese. Set aside.

8. Preheat oven to 350 degrees.

9. Place tortillas on a sheet pan (doing as many as you can at once without overlapping tortillas). Spray both sides of tortilla lightly with cooking spray. Put tortillas in oven for 45 seconds to warm up and make them pliable.

10. Spread 1 cup enchilada sauce on the bottom of a 9x13-inch pan.

11. Place ¾ cup chicken mixture in middle of tortilla and roll up and place on top of spread sauce. You should be able to fit 8 rolled tortillas in your pan.

12. Spoon another ¼ cup tomato sauce down the center of the rolled tortillas and garnish with cheese.

13. Cover baking dish with foil. Bake enchiladas until heated through and cheese is melted, about 10–15 minutes.

14. Uncover and serve immediately with your favorite toppings.

TURKEY CHILE VERDE

SERVES 10–12

1 yellow onion, chopped

1 green pepper, chopped

1 large celery stalk, thickly diced

¼ cup Canola oil

1½ tablespoons garlic, chopped

1 tablespoon dried oregano

4 cups cooked turkey breast, chunked

2 (4-ounce) cans diced chiles

1 (7-ounce) can Herdez green salsa

6¼ cups chicken stock

1 (15-ounce) can white beans, drained and rinsed

¼ cup cilantro, chopped

2 tablespoons lime juice

salt and pepper to taste

1. Sauté vegetables in oil for 5 minutes, then add garlic and oregano. Stir and cook another couple of minutes.

2. Add turkey breast, canned chiles and Herdez green salsa.

3. Add chicken stock and stir.

4. Let simmer for about 15–20 minutes (not boiling) so flavors blend together.

5. To finish, add white beans, chopped cilantro and lime juice. Salt and pepper to taste.

CHILE RELLENOS CASSEROLE

SERVES 10–12

- 6 fresh poblano peppers
- 2 cups pepper Jack cheese, grated
- 2 cups Cheddar cheese, grated
- 5 eggs, beaten
- 1 cup heavy cream
- 4 tablespoons flour
- 1 cup milk
- ½ can Rotel tomato sauce, drained (I like the one with lime and cilantro)
- 3 tablespoons feta
- 2 tablespoons cilantro, chopped

1. Preheat oven 400 degrees.

2. Place poblanos on a sheet pan and roast in the oven for 15 minutes, turn over and continue to roast until skins turn black.

3. Remove from oven.

4. Place poblanos in a plastic bag to steam until cool enough to handle, and then remove skins gently, slice open, seed the peppers.

5. Prepare 9x13-inch baking dish by coating with cooking spray.

6. Chop the peppers and put half of them in the baking dish.

7. Layer with half of the cheeses and then put the other half of the chopped peppers on top of the cheese. Finally, cover with the remaining cheeses.

8. In a bowl, mix the flour, milk and cream.

9. In a separate bowl, beat the eggs; combine with milk mixture, whisking thoroughly.

10. Pour the egg mixture over the top of the chile peppers.

11. Turn the oven down to 350 degrees.

12. Place the baking dish in the oven for approximately 25 minutes.

13. Remove and spoon the tomato sauce over the top.

14. Sprinkle with feta.

15. Bake for another 5–10 minutes, remove and garnish with the cilantro. Serve warm.

GRILLED VEGETABLES

SERVES 8–10

½ red onion, cut into 1-inch slices along the grain

3 sweet bell peppers (1 each red, yellow and orange), de-seeded and stemmed and sliced into 1½- to 2-inch strips

1 each yellow squash and zucchini

1 small eggplant, trimmed, halved lengthwise and sliced along the bias into 1-inch pieces

16 asparagus spears, trimmed

¾ cup Herb Oil (See recipe page 54)

3 carrots, peeled, trimmed, halved lengthwise and sliced along the bias into ½-inch pieces

2 tablespoons olive oil

salt and pepper to taste

1. Heat an outdoor grill on medium to high (or we love to use our grill pan).

2. Toss red onion, peppers, yellow squash, zucchini, asparagus and eggplant in a bowl along with herb oil and season with salt and pepper.

3. Grill 3–4 minutes per side.

4. Preheat oven to 400 degrees.

5. Toss the carrots in a bowl with olive oil and season with salt and pepper. Place carrot slices on a sheet pan and roast in the oven for 10–12 minutes.

6. Toss vegetables together and serve warm or allow to cool and place individually on a platter to serve room temperature with Oven-Dried Tomato Aioli (See recipe page 109).

NEW THREE BEAN SALAD

SERVES 8–10

1½ cups frozen, thawed and shelled edamame

¼ cup olive oil

1 teaspoon ground cumin

1 (15-ounce) can black beans, drained and rinsed

1 (15-ounce) can black eyed peas, drained and rinsed

½ cup red onion, chopped

2 cups celery, diced

2 tablespoons fresh lime juice

½ cup fresh cilantro, chopped

1 pinch garlic, chopped

1½ teaspoons salt

¼ teaspoon black pepper

1. Toss vegetables together.

2. Refrigerate for 30 minutes.

3. Serve chilled.

SUMMER BERRY PIES
MAKES 1 DOUBLE CRUST PIE

2¼ cups flour

2 teaspoons sugar

1 teaspoon salt

1 cup vegetable shortening, chilled

½ cup unsalted butter, chilled

6 tablespoons ice cold water
(a little more if too dry)

CRUST

1. In the bowl of an electric mixer, using the paddle attachment, mix flour, sugar and salt.

2. Add half of the shortening, blending into flour. Then add the rest of the shortening and the butter. The pie crust should look like a coarse meal.

3. Add the cold water a tablespoon at a time to keep the dough moist. Mix until just blended together.

4. On a floured surface, divide the dough into two sections. Flatten each slightly and refrigerate for at least 30 minutes.

4 cups fresh berries

2 tablespoons flour

⅓ cup sugar

1 tablespoon lemon zest, finely chopped

⅛ teaspoon cinnamon

FILLING

1. Combine all the ingredients in a medium mixing bowl and gentle stir until well combined.

6. On a floured surface, roll out the chilled pie dough.

7. Lay crust on top of a 9-inch round pie tin, leaving enough of the crust to hang about an inch over the edge.

8. Fill the crust with the berry filling.

9. Roll out the second piece of chilled dough and place on top of the filling. Crimp the sides of the dough and slice steam vents on the top of the pie.

10. Preheat an oven to 425 degrees. Place the pie on the lower rack and bake for 30 minutes.

11. Reduce oven temperature to 350 degrees and cook for another 25–35 minutes until the crust is golden and berry juice bubbles up through the steam vents.

12. Remove and cool completely on a rack.

SUMMER GARDEN PARTY

Evie Cranston

On July 5th, my good friend and longtime client, Evie Cranston, had a group of girlfriends visit her for several days of fun. Besides hiking, fishing, shopping and Lord knows what else those girls were up to, they had a wonderful dinner at Evie's beautiful home on the Yellowstone River. Almost a decade ago, in nearly the same spot, I catered her daughter Catherine and son-in-law Jeff Vermillion's wedding. This home and backyard remain one of my favorites.

The girls enjoyed one of Evie's favorite meals of Chicken Torte Milanese with Tomato Basil Sauce and Caesar Salad and finished with Fresh Berries with Prosecco Sabayon Sauce. They started out the meal with peppadews filled with Boursin cheese, my famous Smoked Trout Dip on Raincoast Crisp Crackers and Prosciutto-Phyllo Wrapped Asparagus.

Menu

Chicken Torte Milanese with
Tomato Basil Sauce

Caesar Salad

Smoked Trout Dip

Prosciutto-Phyllo Wrapped
Asparagus

Boursin-Filled Peppadews

Fresh Berries with
Prosecco Sabayon Sauce

· · · · Always the gracious hostess, Evie Cranston sets her table for a casually elegant garden party along the Yellowstone River. Chicken Torte Milanese with a Tomato Basil Sauce. Smoked Trout Dip in quenelles on hearty crackers. Classic Caesar Salad.

The perfect setting. Boursin-Filled Peppadews. A toast to the hostess and a midsummer's dream. Prosciutto-Phyllo Wrapped Asparagus.

CHICKEN TORTE MILANESE

SERVES 8–10

6 (6-ounce) herb grilled chicken breasts (See recipe page 54) diced into 2-inch chunks

8 cups shredded Italian cheese mix (mozzarella, Parmesan and Fontina)

2 cups cooked spinach, squeezed of excess moisture

3 cups roasted mushrooms, squeezed of excess moisture (See recipe page 106)

4 cups quartered artichoke hearts, squeezed of excess moisture

3 cups canned roasted red peppers, drained, dried with paper towels and diced

For Egg Wash

1 egg

2 teaspoons water

½ teaspoon dried Italian seasoning

1. Prepare a 9 x 12-inch pan by rubbing it lightly with butter.

2. Mix egg and water for an egg wash; set aside.

3. Cut chilled dough in half. You will use only one half for this recipe; wrap the other half in plastic and freeze for up to 2 months. Divide remaining dough in half and roll out one for bottom layer of the pan and the other for top of torte. Use flour on both sides while rolling out so as to not stick to the surface.

4. Gently lay the rolled dough into the pan. Push dough into pan so it fits into bottom and sides; leave enough hanging off the sides to roll an edge over top layer.

5. Layer one at a time: meat, cheese, spinach, cheese, mushrooms, cheese, artichoke hearts, cheese, roasted red peppers, cheese, pressing down on each cheese layer to pack evenly.

6. Using remaining dough, roll out a top for the torte. Place over layered ingredients, leaving a little hanging over sides. Trim any excess of both layers, but leave enough to fold over crust. Reserve trimmed excess dough.

7. Preheat oven to 375 degrees.

8. Pinch dough together and roll around the edge of the torte. Pinch or press your finger into crust to make it more decorative.

9. With remaining dough, roll out and cut about 6 "leaves" and put on top of the torte. Make 5 or 6 small air slits on top and an "x" in the middle for venting. Brush top and leaves with egg wash. Sprinkle with dried Italian seasonings.

10. Bake for about 45 minutes, or until crust is brown and an internal temperature of about 130 degrees is reached.

11. Let sit 15–20 minutes before cutting. Serve with warmed Tomato Basil Sauce (see recipe page 74).

Torte Dough

MAKES ENOUGH FOR 2 TORTES

- 4 cups all-purpose flour
- 1½ cups salted butter
- ¾ cups ice water

1. Place flour into bowl of electric mixer with paddle attachment. Mix for 1 minute to aerate.

2. Add butter a little at a time until mixture resembles a course meal.

3. Add water a little at a time, mixing until dough pulls away from paddle and forms a ball.

4. Flatten dough to a disk, cover in plastic wrap and chill until firm; 45 minutes to 1 hour.

Tomato Basil Sauce

- 1 tablespoon olive oil
- 1 teaspoon garlic, chopped
- 2 (14-ounce) cans of diced tomatoes, drained
- 1 tablespoon balsamic vinegar
- 1 teaspoon dried basil
- 2 tablespoons fresh basil, chiffonade
- salt and pepper to taste

1. Pour olive oil into a small sauce pan over medium heat. After 30 seconds or so, add the chopped garlic. Stir garlic a few seconds and add the drained tomatoes, balsamic vinegar and dried basil.

2. Let simmer for 10–15 minutes.

3. Remove the sauce from heat and add the fresh basil, salt and pepper.

CAESAR DRESSING

MAKES APPROXIMATELY 4 CUPS

juice of 2 lemons

3 tablespoons garlic, chopped

½ cup shredded Parmesan

2 tablespoons Worcestershire Sauce

3 tablespoons Dijon mustard

3½ cups mayonnaise

salt and pepper to taste

1. Whisk dressing ingredients together until well combined.

2. Season to taste with salt and pepper.

3. Toss 1 cup of dressing with romaine lettuce, top with croutons.

SMOKED TROUT DIP

MAKES 1 ¾ CUPS

½ lb. smoked trout

¼ cup (2 ounces) cream cheese

½ cup heavy cream

1 tablespoon capers

1 tablespoon fresh dill, chopped

1½ tablespoons marinated red onions (See recipe page 105), diced

2 teaspoons wasabi paste

1. Place all ingredients into a stand mixer with a metal whisk.

2. Whip until ingredients come together into a mousse-like consistency.

3. Serve with hearty multi-grain crackers. I love serving it with Raincoast Crisp; these fig and olive crackers are available at Livingston's Gourmet Cellar and other gourmet shops.

PROSCIUTTO-PHYLLO WRAPPED ASPARAGUS

SERVES 12

- 1 package Pepperidge Farms Phyllo, thawed
- ¾ cup melted butter
- ½ cup Pecorino-Romano cheese, finely grated
- 12 thin slices of prosciutto, cut in half
- 24 asparagus spears (choose thicker as opposed to thinner), trim to 4 inches long

1. Preheat oven to 400 degrees.

2. Line a baking sheet with parchment paper.

3. Place two sheets of phyllo dough on a dry surface keeping the other sheets covered with a slightly damp towel.

4. Brush phyllo with melted butter and cut phyllo sheets in half horizontally and then into fourths vertically so you have 8 pieces all together.

5. Sprinkle phyllo with 2 tablespoons grated cheese, then place one piece of prosciutto on each square.

6. Arrange one piece of asparagus on the bottom edge of each square and carefully roll phyllo around asparagus, making sure the tip of the asparagus is "peeking" through.

7. Brush with additional butter and sprinkle with a little more cheese. Repeat with the remaining asparagus.

8. This can be made one day in advance if tightly wrapped with plastic wrap and refrigerated.

9. Bake the rolled spears until golden brown, 8–10 minutes. Serve warm.

BOURSIN-FILLED PEPPADEWS

SERVES 10–12

- 1 dozen firm peppadews, drained of excess juice
- ½ cup, plus 1½ tablespoons Boursin cheese, room temperature

1. Fill a pastry bag with 12-inch floret tip, with Boursin, using a rubber spatula.

2. Gently pipe Boursin into peppadews until a ½-inch floret tops the pepper.

3. Chill and serve on a platter.

FRESH BERRIES WITH A PROSECCO SABAYON SAUCE

SERVES 8–10

- 4 egg yolks
- ¼ cup sugar
- ¾ cup Prosecco
- 2 tablespoons kirsch
- 8 cups assorted fresh berries

1. Whisk the egg yolks and the sugar together in the top part of a double boiler over boiling water, until foamy. Make sure the bowl doesn't touch the boiling water, or your eggs will curdle.

2. Add the Prosecco and whisk constantly until thick and creamy, about 10–12 minutes.

3. Remove from the heat and whisk in the kirsch.

4. Allow to cool for about 15 minutes.

5. Serve chilled in glass bowls with fresh berries.

RIVERSIDE RENDEZVOUS

Menu

Angel Hair Pasta Salad

Shrimp and Avocado Salad
with Dijon Shallot Vinaigrette

Tuna Pasta Salad

Broccoli Grape Salad

Quinoa Tabouleh

Tarragon Chicken Salad

Noodles in Peanut Sauce

Curried Couscous Salad

John Taliaferro and Malou Flato

We always know when summer starts and ends by the arrival and departure of good friends John Taliaferro and Malou Flato. Without a doubt, the writer and artist duo rank among our retail store's best customers. Tugging cooler in hand, they will clean out our deli case of salads to make sure they are well equipped to enjoy a day or two of hiking and, of course, a lively game of bridge with longtime pals Julie and Hannibal Anderson.

Heading down the trail. Shuffling the deck for a game of bridge. Curried Couscous Salad. Digging in.

Visiting on the cabin deck. Shrimp and Avocado Salad along with a variety of other chilled salad favorites in assorted jars. John Taliaferro and Hannibal bird watching. Broccoli and Grape Salad. Malou leads the march home from the river.

ANGEL HAIR PASTA SALAD

SERVES 8

½ lb. angel hair pasta

4 cups grape tomatoes

⅓ cup green onions

½ teaspoon fresh garlic clove, finely minced

⅓ cup fresh basil, packed and chiffonade

2 tablespoons flat leaf parsley, chopped

⅓ cup olive oil

1½ tablespoons feta cheese, crumbled

1. Cook pasta according to package instructions. Set aside.

2. Cut tomatoes in half (in fourths if they are bigger). Trim green onion tops and slice whites on the bias.

3. Combine all the ingredients (except cheese) in a large bowl, toss thoroughly. Garnish with crumbled goat cheese.

4. Serve hot or cold, as desired (we serve it chilled in the shop).

SHRIMP AND AVOCADO SALAD

SERVES 8–10

2 lbs. of medium-sized shrimp, peeled, deveined and cooked

2 avocados, diced

⅓ cup red onion, diced

1 cup celery, diced

2 tablespoons parsley, chopped

2 tablespoons dill, chopped

1 dash of Tabasco

1 cup Dijon Shallot Vinaigrette (enough to coat nicely) (recipe follows)

salt and pepper to taste

1. Gently toss all ingredients on a bed of greens and chill before serving.

Tuna Pasta Salad

SERVES 6

1 lb. of bowtie pasta

2 (7-ounce) cans tuna, drained and left chunky

1 celery stalk, diced

2 tablespoons red onion, diced

1½ tablespoons cornichons, diced

1½ tablespoons fresh dill, chopped

4 tablespoons fresh flat leaf parsley, chopped

⅓ cup plain yogurt

⅓ cup lemon juice

1⅓ cups mayonnaise (Hellmann's or Best Foods)

salt and pepper

1. Cook pasta according to package instructions. Set aside.

2. Gently toss all ingredients until well combined.

3. Refrigerate before serving.

Dijon Shallot Vinaigrette

MAKES 1 CUP

2 shallots, diced

⅓ cup white wine vinegar

⅔ cup Dijon mustard

1½ cups olive oil

salt and pepper to taste

1. Mix all ingredients, then gradually whisk in olive oil to blend. Season with salt and pepper.

2. Toss with mixed greens and top with candied nuts.

BROCCOLI GRAPE SALAD

SERVES 8–8

2 cups of mayonnaise
(Hellmann's or Best Foods)

½ cup apple cider vinegar

¾ cup plus 2 tablespoons
sugar

1½ lbs. fresh broccoli, cut
into bite-sized pieces

2 cups red grapes,
destemmed

½ cup celery, diced

½ cup toasted almonds

½ cup golden raisins

DRESSING

1. Place mayonnaise, vinegar and sugar in a mixing bowl and whisk together until sugar is dissolved completely.

SALAD

1. In a large bowl, toss salad ingredients with 4 cups Broccoli Dressing until broccoli is thoroughly coated.

QUINOA TABOULEH

SERVES 6

1 cup quinoa, cooked per
directions and cooled

½ English cucumber, diced

¾ cup Roma tomato,
deseeded and diced

2 green onions, sliced

½ cup parsley, diced

2 teaspoons garlic, diced

6 tablespoons (3 ounces)
lemon juice

2 tablespoons olive oil

salt and pepper to taste

1. Toss cooled quinoa with remaining ingredients until well-combined.

2. Chill and serve.

TARRAGON CHICKEN SALAD

SERVES 6–8

- 4 (6-ounce) chicken breasts
- 1 cup heavy cream
- ½ cup sour cream
- ½ cup mayonnaise
- 2 ribs celery, diced chunky
- 2 tablespoons fresh tarragon, chopped
- ½ cup toasted walnuts, coarsely chopped
- salt and pepper to taste

1. Preheat oven to 350 degrees.

2. Arrange chicken breasts skin-side up on a baking sheet and cover with heavy cream.

3. Bake for 20–25 minutes.

4. Remove from oven and allow to cool in the cream.

5. When cooled, shred the meat into bite-size pieces and transfer to a bowl. Discard the cream.

6. Whisk the sour cream and mayonnaise together in a bowl. Add the celery, walnuts, tarragon, salt and pepper and toss well. Pour over the shredded chicken.

7. Cover and refrigerate for at least 4 hours or overnight. Adjust seasoning to taste before serving.

NOODLES IN PEANUT SAUCE

SERVES 6–8

- ½ lb. spaghetti noodles, cooked
- 2 small peppers, red and yellow, julienned
- 1 carrot, julienned
- ¼ cup green onions, sliced

- ½ cup soy sauce
- ½ cup peanut butter
- ⅓ cup Canola oil
- 2 tablespoons each sesame oil, chili garlic sauce
- 1 tablespoon sugar
- ¼ cup cilantro, chopped

NOODLES

1. Cook spaghetti according to package instructions. Set aside.

2. Prepare vegetables.

PEANUT SAUCE

1. Whisk all ingredients in a bowl until it's a creamy and smooth consistency.

2. Toss with noodles and vegetables until well-coated.

3. Portion out and top with chopped peanuts.

CURRIED COUSCOUS SALAD

SERVES 6–8

1½ cups couscous, cooked

1 tablespoon butter

1½ cups boiling water

½ cup yogurt

¼ cup olive oil

1 teaspoon white wine vinegar

1 teaspoon curry powder

¼ teaspoon tumeric

1½ teaspoons salt

1 teaspoon black pepper

½ cup carrot, grated

½ cup parsley, minced

½ cup dried currants

¼ cup toasted almonds, blanched

2 green onions, thinly sliced

¼ cup red onion, finely diced

1. Combine couscous and butter top with boiling water and cover with plastic wrap until softened.

2. Mix cooked couscous with remaining ingredients. Adjust moisture and seasoning to taste.

FAMILY FEAST

Kathryn and John Heminway

Menu

Crab Cakes with Chili-Lime Sauce

Carrot Ginger Soup

Fresh Spring Rolls
with Asian Dipping Sauce

Evil Jungle Chicken with Perfect Rice

Snappy Lemon Ginger Tea Ice Cream

Author and documentary filmmaker John Heminway has been a loyal client for years. He and his wife Kathryn have traveled and worked around the world, but Montana is home base. Their rustic "camp" at Cloud Ranch has become a family treasure. Kathryn's rare talent for finding one-of-a-kind pieces to fill their home never ceases to amaze me.

Time on the ranch seems to stand still and the Heminways keep things simple there — flying kites, horseback riding, reading, time with friends. They always stop at Mustang on their way from Bozeman to Cloud to have a fun family weekend.

· · · · Simple ingredients for an elegant garnish. A seat in the shade awaits. Lucia and John Heminway share a moment before the fun begins. Crab Cakes with Chili-Lime Sauce. Kite-flying before the feast.

The Heminway dining room is a cool respite on a hot summer day. A sip of wine after lunch at Big Timber Creek Falls with John Heminway and friends. Evil Jungle Chicken. Kathryn and daughter Lucia walking back to the house.

CRAB CAKES WITH CHILI-LIME SAUCE

SERVES 6

- 1 can of lump crab meat
- 1 egg
- ¾ cup panko (plus extra for dredging of cake)
- ¼ cup mayonnaise
- 2 tablespoons Dijon mustard
- 2 dashes of Tabasco
- 2 dashes of Worcestershire Sauce
- 2 tablespoons flat leaf parsley, chopped
- 3 green onions, chopped (I like to use a little bit of the green as well)
- 1 cup Canola oil

1. Gently mix all of the ingredients, except oil.

2. Form into 12 cakes and dredge in extra panko. Cakes should be about 1-inch thick and 3 inches around. Chill for 15–20 minutes in the refrigerator before frying.

3. Pour oil in a small sauté pan. Oil should go about one-quarter of the way up the side of the pan. Add a little extra if needed.

4. Brown cakes a few at a time. Cook 5 minutes per side. Be careful not to overcrowd cakes in the pan. Use a slotted spatula (I like the fish spatulas) to remove cakes onto a drying rack or paper towel to drain excess oil.

CHILI-LIME SAUCE

MAKES APPROXIMATELY 2 CUPS

- 1½ cups mayonnaise
- 1 shallot finely diced
- ¼ cup fresh squeezed lime juice
- ½ tablespoon chili garlic sauce
- ⅓ cup cilantro, chopped

1. Mix ingredients in a bowl with a whisk until well combined.

CARROT GINGER SOUP

SERVES 8

12 medium carrots, peeled and trimmed

2 inches fresh ginger root, peeled and sliced thin

2 tablespoons honey

1½ teaspoons salt

½ teaspoon pepper

¼ teaspoon dried ginger

1. Cut carrots lengthwise, then in half to expose sweet center of carrot.

2. Place carrots and ginger in 6 cups of water in a stock pot. Bring to a boil and simmer 30 minutes or until carrots are soft.

3. Purée the carrots, ginger, water, honey, salt, pepper and additional dried ginger in blender and strain through a sieve. Serve hot or cold.

PERFECT RICE

SERVES 8

2 cups basmati rice

4½ cups water

1 teaspoon Canola oil

2 tablespoons fresh cilantro sprigs

4 green onions, sliced on the bias

salt and pepper to taste

1. Over medium-high heat, bring the water, basmati rice and oil to a boil.

2. Turn heat down so water simmers and let cook for about 7 minutes, stirring a couple of times. When most of the water is absorbed, turn the heat off and cover pot slightly.

3. When rice is done, place into a bowl; season with salt and pepper and sprinkle with cilantro and green onions.

Fresh Spring Rolls with Asian Dipping Sauce

MAKES APPROXIMATELY 2 CUPS

4 rice paper wrappers
(Sold in Asian food aisle in
supermarkets.)

½ cup cooked shrimp

¼ cup carrot shredded

½ cup mixed greens

12 sections of canned
mandarin oranges,
drained of juice

½ an avocado cut into
4 slices

1 green onion, cut into fourths
lengthwise

16 cilantro leaves

16 mint leaves

1 cup rice noodles or
cellophane noodles, soaked
in hot water until translucent
(about 5 minutes)

1. One at a time, soak rice paper in warm water and blot dry with a paper towel. Place each of the ingredients evenly on top of each of the four rice papers and roll up from bottom, tucking in the sides half way through so roll is completely closed.

2. Wrap in plastic and refrigerate for about 1 hour before cutting into thirds.

3. Serve with Asian Dipping Sauce.

Asian Dipping Sauce

MAKES APPROXIMATELY 3 ½ CUPS

2 cups of rice wine vinegar

½ cup lime juice

½ cup shallots, finely diced

¼ cup cilantro, chopped

2 tablespoons jalapeños,
chopped

2 tablespoons sugar

1. Mix ingredients in a mixing bowl.

EVIL JUNGLE CHICKEN

SERVES 8

4 tablespoons Canola oil

6 (5-ounce) chicken breasts, cubed

2 tablespoons each of chopped lemongrass, garlic, ginger root

2 tablespoons red curry paste

3 colored sweet bell peppers, seeded and sliced lengthwise

3 medium-sized carrots, peeled and sliced on the bias

3 cans coconut milk

½ cup soy sauce

6 tablespoons peanut butter

2 tablespoons chili garlic sauce

1½ cups sugar snap peas

3 tablespoons fresh basil, chiffonade

1. Heat oil in a pan on medium-high.

2. Brown chicken in oil and remove with a slotted spoon.

3. Using the same pan, add lemongrass, garlic, ginger root and curry paste and stir to mix. Then add peppers and carrots. Stir over medium heat until slightly softened.

4. Add coconut milk, soy sauce and peanut butter. Stir again until thoroughly combined. Add browned chicken, peas and chili garlic sauce.

5. Add basil at the very end just before serving.

6. Serve with Perfect Rice (See recipe page 94).

 *Kitchen Dish*

Do not over crowd your meat when browning. If necessary do it in batches. The end result will be a more tender meat.

SNAPPY LEMON GINGER TEA ICE CREAM

MAKES 1 QUART

- 1 cup whole milk
- ¾ cup sugar
- pinch of salt
- 1 rounded tablespoon of Tumblewood Tea Snappy Lemon Ginger Tea leaves
- 2 cups of heavy cream
- 6 large egg yolks

1. Bring milk, sugar, salt and tea leaves to a simmer, being careful not to burn the milk. Remove from heat.

2. Pour cream into a mixing bowl with a mesh strainer over it. In a separate medium-sized bowl, whisk together egg yolks. Slowly pour the warm mixture into the egg yolks, whisking constantly. Scrape the warm mixture back into the sauce pan. Stir mixture constantly over medium heat with a heat-proof spatula, scraping bottom as you stir until mixture coats the back of the spatula to form a custard.

3. Pour custard through strainer, pressing the mixture to extract the liquid; then stir into cream, whisking vigorously until custard is frothy.

4. Stir until cool over an ice bath. It's important to cool liquid completely to allow the tea to diffuse its flavor. When cooled, add the mixture to your ice cream maker and follow maker's instructions.

Kitchen Dish

If you don't own a lemon juicer, use a fork to get the most juice out of lemons and limes. Holding the lemon by the skin side in one hand, take the fork in the other and use it to "dig" into the flesh of the lemon. Squeeze over a bowl, then strain juice into a storable container. Refrigerate it up to two weeks or freeze it.

A Fisherman's Lunch

Lee Kinsey

Fishing guide extraordinaire Lee Kinsey successfully transitioned from a possible engineering career one day to buying a boat and making his dream of becoming a fly fishing guide a reality the next. His clients are some of the most respected people in the country and are committed to his guidance on the rivers and spring creeks all over Montana. My bet is that Lee could fish anywhere, but his favorite "home water" is surely DePuy Spring Creek. Just a short drive south of Livingston, this private stream seems like a world away. We are so pleased to have become friends with Lee and his wife Abby and to see his smiling face every morning from April to October, when he picks up these lunches for the perfect streamside picnic.

Menu

Cucumber Mint Soup

Gazpacho

Italian Muffeletta Sandwich

Roast Beef Sandwich

Secret Sauces:
Oven-Dried Tomato Aioli
Turkey Dressing
Blue Cheese Mayonnaise

Fisherman's favorite: Italian Muffeletta Sandwich. Montana Boatbuilders'
custom drift boat is always at the ready for a day on the river. Eva's Cabin,
fishing hut and secret spot for anglers in the know. Lunch on the go.

. . . . Lee Kinsey and friends read the water on DePuy Spring Creek. Trout cookies. Cucumber Mint Soup and Gazpacho from Mustang, of course! Lee Kinsey finds secluded waters.

CUCUMBER MINT SOUP
MAKES APPROXIMATELY 8 CUPS

3 English cucumbers washed, trimmed of ends and cut into chunks

¾ cup yogurt

¾ cup heavy cream

¾ cup fresh lemon juice

¾ cup fresh mint leaves

½ teaspoon dried cumin

1 teaspoon salt

½ teaspoon pepper

½ cup vegetable stock

1. Purée all ingredients in batches in blender.

2. Refrigerate for at least one hour.

3. Serve chilled.

GAZPACHO
MAKES APPROXIMATELY 8 CUPS

3 lbs. of vine ripened tomatoes, cut into chunks

1 English cucumber, cut into chunks

1 colored pepper, cut into chunks

1 shallot, chopped

½ cup red onion, chopped

2 tablespoons cilantro, chopped

2 cups V-8 juice

4 tablespoons balsamic vinegar

4 dashes of Tabasco

2 teaspoons salt

1 teaspoon black pepper

2 tablespoons sour cream (for garnish)

1. Combine all ingredients in a medium mixing bowl.

2. In batches of 2–3 cups, put ingredients in blender and purée for 10–15 seconds.

3. Refrigerate for at least one hour.

4. Serve chilled with a dollop of sour cream on top of each serving.

ITALIAN MUFFELETTA SANDWICH

SERVES 6

1 package Good Seasons
Italian Dressing Mix

1 cup Dijon mustard

1 cup mayonnaise

ITALIAN DRESSING

1. Follow instructions for dressing mix and then whisk in Dijon and mayonnaise.

1 cup red onion, diced

2 tablespoons rice wine
vinegar

MARINATED RED ONIONS

1. Place diced red onion in a bowl and cover with rice wine vinegar.

2. Let marinate for about one hour.

3. Drain the juice before putting onions on the sandwiches.

¼ cup roasted red peppers,
diced

¼ cup pepperoncinis, diced

¼ cup green olives, diced

STUFFELETTA

1. Mix red peppers, pepperoncinis and green olives thoroughly and reserve.

assorted Italian meats

ciabatta bread

SANDWICH ASSEMBLY

1. Spread Stuffeletta (the name Dan made up for all the "stuff" in the sandwich) on both sides of bread. To assemble sandwich, layer assorted Italian meats with sliced provolone cheese, marinated red onions, fresh basil, mixed greens and Italian dressing onto one slice of the Stuffeletta-covered, grilled ciabatta bread. Top with second piece of Stuffeletta-covered ciabatta.

ROAST BEEF SANDWICH

SERVES 8

2½ lbs. sirloin tip, roasted

2 tablespoons garlic, chopped

1 teaspoon dried Italian seasoning

2 teaspoons salt

1 teaspoon pepper

4 tablespoons olive oil

ROAST BEEF

1. Spread ingredients over beef sirloin completely. Roast in 375-degree oven for about 35–45 minutes for medium rare.

2. Let stand for 15 minutes before slicing.

1 large yellow onion, diced

2 tablespoons olive oil

CARAMELIZED ONIONS

1. Heat oil in sauté pan over medium-high heat.

2. Add onions and stir occasionally so onions don't burn onto the bottom of the pan. Cook until onions turn a caramelized color.

1 lb. medium button mushrooms

2 tablespoons olive oil

¼ teaspoon salt

⅛ teaspoon pepper

ROASTED MUSHROOMS

1. Preheat oven to 375 degrees.

2. Clean, trim and slice mushrooms.

3. Place mushrooms on a sheet pan with olive oil, salt and pepper. Toss to coat.

4. Roast mushrooms in an oven for 10–15 minutes.

ciabatta bread or your favorite rolls

8 slices Jarlsberg cheese

2 tomatoes, sliced

¼ cup Dijon mustard

SANDWICH ASSEMBLY

1. Place sliced beef on bottom of bread topped with caramelized onions, mushrooms and sliced Jarlsberg cheese.

2. Put in preheated 375-degree oven for 6-8 minutes or until cheese is melted. Top with sliced tomatoes, romaine and Dijon mustard.

OVEN-DRIED TOMATO AIOLI

MAKES 2 CUPS

2 lbs. Roma Tomatoes cut into sixths

½ teaspoon salt

½ teaspoon pepper

1 teaspoon dried Italian seasoning

2 tablespoons olive oil

1 teaspoon garlic, chopped

1 cup mayonnaise (Hellmann's or Best Foods)

½ teaspoon salt

¼ teaspoon pepper

1. Preheat oven to 300 degrees.

2. Spray the bottom of a sheet pan with cooking spray.

3. Place tomatoes seed side up on pan. Sprinkle with salt, pepper and Italian seasoning evenly. Drizzle with olive oil.

4. Roast in oven for 3 hours.

5. Turn oven off and let tomatoes sit in oven overnight.

6. When cool, place tomatoes in a bowl of a food processor along with garlic. Process for 15–20 seconds and then add mayonnaise and salt and pepper.

TURKEY DRESSING

MAKES 3 CUPS

¾ cup Dijon mustard

1 cup mayonnaise

1 cup maple syrup

1. Mix ingredients in a bowl.

BLUE CHEESE MAYONNAISE

6 CUPS

1½ lbs. blue cheese, crumbled

3½ cups mayonnaise

1. Stir together.

2. Keep refrigerated until ready to use.

A Prairie Picnic

Menu

Bison Chili Molé

Pico de Gallo

Guacamole

Corn Salad

Caramel Walnut Brownies

World Wildlife Fund

WWF is a global organization that protects wild places around the world — including right here at home in the Northern Great Plains. WWF works here to ensure that thriving prairies and wildlife contribute to the vibrance of communities.

In September 2012, I was asked to create a picnic for WWF's International Conservation Committee. Conservation leaders from across the globe had come to the Charles M. Russell National Wildlife Refuge in eastern Montana to view the annual elk rut. This gathering of hundreds of mating elk by the Missouri River is one of the region's most incredible wildlife sightings.

With no running water or electricity, preparing a picnic would be no small effort. My bison and butternut squash chili was the perfect solution. Given the huge tasks WWF takes on, I wanted to provide some hearty Montana nourishment to keep them going.

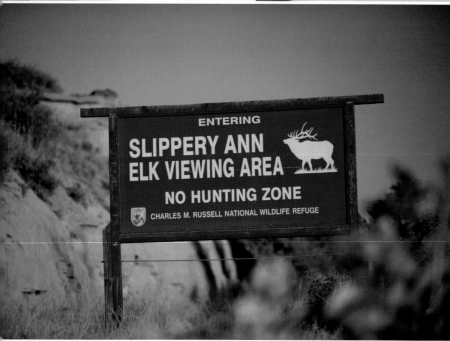

This is roughing it. Caramel Walnut Brownies for all. Thrilled to dine on the prairie. Montana's premiere elk-viewing site. Corn Salad.

Vine-ripened tomatoes make the best Pico de Gallo. Standing room only at dusk on the American Prairie Reserve. Entranced in wildlife watching. Bison Chili Molé. Come `n´ get it!

BISON CHILI MOLÉ
SERVES 10–12

2½ ounces dried ancho chiles

4 lbs. bison stew meat (I actually use 8 lbs. of bison short ribs and trim the meat myself; however, this is quite time consuming)

½ cup Canola oil

4 cups yellow onions, chopped

1 teaspoon kosher salt

½ teaspoon black pepper

2 tablespoons garlic, chopped

2 tablespoons chili powder

1 tablespoon ground cumin

1 tablespoon dried oregano

2 teaspoons coriander

2 teaspoons cinnamon

1 teaspoon kosher salt

3½ cups stock (beef or chicken, I use chicken)

3 teaspoons unsweetened cocoa powder

1 cup canned roasted red peppers, diced

1 (4-ounce) can diced green chiles

2 (14.5-ounce) cans diced tomatoes

1 (12-ounce) can of beer (preferably Mexican)

4 cups butternut squash

2 tablespoons olive oil

⅓ cup cilantro, chopped

¼ cup green onions, sliced

⅔ cup sour cream

1. Place four cups of water in a medium pan. Bring to a boil, add chiles (make sure water covers them) and remove pan from the stove. Sometimes I will place a can or some other heavy object on the chiles to keep them submerged in hot water. Allow to soak at least 30 minutes or until softened.

2. Drain chiles, reserving liquid. Place chiles in a blender and add 1 to 1½ cups of reserved soaking liquid, adding more if too thick.

3. Place a heavy, large pot over medium-high heat. Add Canola oil, and after a minute or so, when oil is hot, add chopped onions and garlic. Stir for about 5 minutes. Season bison stew (or rib) meat with salt and pepper, then add to the cooking onions. Stir bison meat until browned, about 15 to 20 minutes. Once it's browned, add chili powder, cumin seed, oregano, coriander, cinnamon and 2 teaspoons kosher salt. Stir well to coat the meat with all of the spices.

4. Add chicken stock, ancho chile purée, cocoa powder, diced green chiles, diced tomatoes and beer. Stir this and let ingredients simmer slightly covered for 2–3 hours or until meat is completely tender.

5. Next, preheat oven to 375 degrees. Toss the butternut squash in 2 tablespoons olive oil on a baking sheet and season with salt and pepper. Roast in the oven for 20–25 minutes, or just until fork tender. (Do not over bake.) Set aside.

6. Add butternut squash to tender meat mixture, stir and continue to simmer for about 5–10 minutes. Add cilantro just before serving to keep the taste of the cilantro nice a fresh.

7. Top with a sprinkle of green onions and a dollop of sour cream.

PICO DE GALLO

MAKES 4 CUPS

2 lbs. of vine-ripened tomatoes

2 tablespoons cilantro

3 tablespoons lime juice

1 teaspoon garlic, chopped

1 small jalapeño, seeded and finely diced

1 small red pepper, seeded and diced

4 tablespoons red onion, diced

1 teaspoon salt

¼ teaspoon pepper

1 tablespoon rice wine vinegar

1. Using a melon baller, scoop out center of tomatoes, discard and dice remaining tomato into ¼-inch pieces.

2. Mix with all other ingredients and let sit for 30 minutes before serving.

GUACAMOLE

MAKES 2 CUPS

1 lb. of avocados

1 tablespoon rice wine vinegar

¼ teaspoon dried cumin

2 teaspoons fresh lime juice

1½ tablespoons cilantro, chopped

3 thinly slice green onions

¼ teaspoons salt

Pinch of pepper

2 dashes of Tabasco

1. Scoop out avocados and cut into chunks.

2. Add other ingredients into a mixing bowl and with a potato masher, mash ingredients, leaving chunky.

CORN SALAD

SERVES 6–8

2½ lbs. frozen super sweet corn

½ tablespoon garlic, chopped

1 tablespoon Canola oil

¼ cup cilantro, chopped

1 colored sweet pepper, diced

½ small red onion, diced

2 tablespoons, plus 2 teaspoons rice wine vinegar

2 tablespoons, plus 2 teaspoons lime juice

salt and pepper to taste

1. Sauté corn and garlic in olive oil until corn thaws and is softened.

2. Let the corn cool, then add cilantro, peppers, red onion, rice wine vinegar, lime juice. Season with salt and pepper.

3. Serve chilled.

CARAMEL WALNUT BROWNIES

MAKES 1 DOZEN

2 ounces unsweetened chocolate

6 tablespoons butter

2 cups of sugar

4 eggs

1 cup flour

12 ounces wrapped caramels, peeled

¼ cup heavy cream

2 cups walnuts, chopped

1 cup semi-sweet chocolate chips

1. Preheat oven to 350 degrees.

2. Melt unsweetened chocolate and butter in microwave, careful not to burn. When melted, stir in sugar, then eggs. Add flour to the chocolate mix.

3. Prepare a 9x12-inch hotel pan by lining with foil and coating with cooking spray. Pour half of the chocolate batter into the pan, spreading evenly. Bake for 20–25 minutes or until firm to the touch. Let cool for 10 minutes before serving.

4. Combine caramels and heavy cream in a microwave-proof bowl. Melt in microwave for 2–3 minutes; whisk to combine.

5. Spread caramel sauce and 1 cup chopped walnuts onto first layer, then add chocolate chips. Next, spread the remaining chocolate mix on top and top with rest of the walnuts. Bake an additional 25–30 minutes.

A HOLIDAY TRADITION

Jeff and Susan Bridges

We all know Jeff (or as most everyone knows him, "the Dude") to be a fabulous, award-winning actor, but it's his wife Susan with whom I have the North Dakota connection and to whom I have become close. Over the years, her kind words have kept me working the schedule that I do. You can never hear "What would we do without you?" or "You mean so much to us" enough. So Susan, I thank you for your support and encouragement, and I am honored that it is me you call to help make your time here in Montana more special.

Menu

Pancetta-Sage Stuffed
Boneless Turkey

Classic Gravy

Mashed Potatoes

Roasted Root Vegetables

Orange-Cranberry Relish

Apple Spice Cake
with Warm Caramel Sauce

· · · · Two-fingers and a plate-full, if you please. Elegant table settings for a traditional occasion. Roasted Root Vegetables. The family gathering.

···· Pancetta-Sage Stuffed Boneless Turkey. A Montana getaway. Apple Spice Cake with Warm Caramel Sauce. Fresh sage tucked into the pancetta adds an extra layer of flavor to the turkey.

PANCETTA-SAGE STUFFED BONELESS TURKEY

SERVES 6–8

1 (6-lb.) boneless turkey with skin on (or you can use a boneless turkey breast if you just like white meat)

kosher salt and fresh ground pepper

½ lb. pancetta, thinly sliced

6 fresh sage leaves

2 tablespoons unsalted butter

1. Set the whole turkey open, skin-side down on top of a piece of plastic wrap. Place another piece of plastic wrap on top of the turkey and flatten it to an even thickness with a meat pounder.

2. Season the turkey with salt and pepper and evenly spread the stuffing (see recipe, next page) over the meat.

3. Beginning on one side, roll the turkey into a compact roast.

4. Place pancetta slices around turkey, tucking the slices underneath as well.

5. Tie the turkey with kitchen string in four to five places, evenly spaced apart. Season the turkey with salt and pepper.

6. Place fresh sage leaves under kitchen string and dot the outside of the turkey with butter.

7. Roast the turkey in the middle of the oven for 30 minutes, brushing the turkey with the melted butter in the pan. Add an extra cup of liquid if pan is too dry (water or chicken stock will do).

8. Roast for approximately 45 minutes longer or until an instant-read thermometer inserted in the thickest part of the turkey registers 140 degrees. Add more liquid to the pan if necessary.

9. Transfer the turkey to a carving board.

10. Remove kitchen string from turkey and slice into ⅓-inch slices. Arrange the slices on a platter and serve gravy separately.

TURKEY STUFFING

SERVES 6–8

8 ounces pancetta, diced

1 small yellow onion, diced

1 carrot, peeled and diced

1 celery stalk, diced

4 cups ciabatta bread, dried and decrusted cubed in 1-inch pieces

1 tablespoon fresh sage, finely chopped

½ cup chicken stock

salt and pepper to taste

1. In a large sauté pan, brown diced pancetta over medium heat, stirring occasionally, about 8–10 minutes.

2. Add the onions, carrots and celery, stirring until vegetables are softened.

3. Add the cubed bread and fresh sage, stirring to coat.

4. Place bread in a bowl along with chicken stock and allow to cool.

CLASSIC GRAVY

MAKES 6 CUPS

2 tablespoons unsalted butter

2 tablespoons flour

6 cups turkey stock (or chicken stock)

1 tablespoon fresh sage, chopped

1. Melt butter over medium heat in a sauté pan.

2. Whisk in flour and let cook for about 1 minute.

3. Slowly add stock, one cup at a time, along with any juices remaining in turkey roasting pan.

4. Add chopped sage and cook for another 5 minutes.

5. Strain liquid and pour into gravy boat.

MASHED POTATOES

SERVES 6–8

5 lbs. Yukon Gold potatoes

1 tablespoon kosher salt

1 cup of butter melted with
2 cups of heavy cream

1 teaspoon salt

½ teaspoon black pepper

2 tablespoons butter

salt and pepper to taste

1. Peel and cut potatoes into even chunks. Put into a stock pot with enough water to cover. Bring to a boil and add kosher salt.

2. Let potatoes cook on a rolling boil for 20–25 minutes or until potatoes are fork tender.

3. Drain potatoes in a colander.

4. Rice the potatoes into a mixing bowl and add melted butter and cream.

5. With the whisk attachment, whisk on low to medium speed, scraping sides of bowl to make sure potatoes get whipped until creamy. Add salt and pepper to taste.

6. Place potatoes in a 9x13-inch casserole dotted with additional butter and reheat, uncovered, at 375 degrees for 5–10 minutes.

ROASTED ROOT VEGETABLES

SERVES 6–8

1 turnip, peeled and sliced into ½-inch strips

2 parsnips, peeled and sliced into ½-inch strips, about 4 inches long

3 leeks, white parts only, sliced 4 inches long

3 large carrots, peeled and sliced into ½-inch strips, about 4 inches long

2 teaspoons salt

1 teaspoon black pepper

4 tablespoons olive oil

1. Preheat oven to 400 degrees.

2. Mix all of the ingredients in a bowl. Lay vegetables on a sheet pan, being careful not to let vegetables overlap.

3. Roast in oven for 15–20 minutes or until vegetables are fork tender.

ORANGE-CRANBERRY RELISH

MAKES 4 CUPS

- ½ cup candied orange peel
- juice of 1 orange
- 2 cups of water
- 1 Granny Smith apple, peeled, cored and cut into ½-inch chunks
- 1 (12-ounce) bag of fresh cranberries
- 1¼ cup sugar
- ½ teaspoon ground cinnamon
- ¼ teaspoon each ground cloves and ground ginger

1. Combine all of the ingredients in a saucepan over medium to high heat.

2. Bring to a boil, reduce heat to low and simmer gently, stirring occasionally until sauce thickens, about 15 minutes. Orange peel and apples should be tender and cranberries should be softened.

3. Allow to cool before serving.

APPLE SPICE CAKE

SERVES 6-8

- 2 cups of sugar
- 2 eggs
- ½ cup butter
- 2 cups of flour
- 1 teaspoon each cinnamon and nutmeg
- 2 teaspoons baking soda
- 6 apples, chopped fine
- 1 cup nuts (your choice), chopped

CAKE

1. Preheat oven to 375 degrees.

2. Cream sugar, eggs and butter together.

3. Add flour, cinnamon, nutmeg and baking soda.

4. Next, add apples and chopped nuts; fold mixture until all ingredients are combined.

5. Spread batter in a bundt cake pan or a 9x13-inch pan, and serve with Warm Caramel Sauce drizzled over the top.

- ½ cup each brown sugar, white sugar, butter and heavy cream
- 1 teaspoon vanilla
- 1 tablespoon flour

CARAMEL SAUCE

1. Combine all ingredients in a sauce pan.

2. Bring to a boil and cook for two minutes.

SAVOR
THE STORM

Menu

Roasted Butternut Squash Soup

Kalamata-Fig Tapenade

White Bean Roasted Garlic Dip

Cumin-Spiced Carrot Dip

Grilled Foccacia

Grilled Vegetable
and Italian Sausage Lasagna

Carol Guzman
and
Clyde Aspevig

I can't remember if I met artists Clyde Aspevig and Carol Guzman after working with American Prairie Reserve, or if they introduced me to the organization, but they've both become very important clients as well as friends. While Clyde sits on the board of American Prairie Reserve, Carol launched Landsnorkeling.org, a website for like-minded folks to share outdoor experiences, especially with children. After landsnorkeling this fall with some friends, Carol, Clyde and guests enjoyed one of their favorite meals picked up at Mustang.

Gathering around the table. Roasted Butternut Squash Soup. Grilled Vegetable and Italian Sausage Lasagna. The first snow blows in.

Kalamata-Fig Tapenade, White Bean Roasted Garlic Dip and Cumin-Spiced Carrot Dip. Returning from land snorkeling along the Shields River. Cheers to a warm and cozy night! Jeffrey Schutz and Charlotte Caldwell.

ROASTED BUTTERNUT SQUASH SOUP

SERVES 6–8

- 4 butternut squash
- ¼ cup brown sugar
- 4 tablespoons butter
- 4 cups chicken or vegetable stock
- 2 potatoes
- 1 carrot
- 1 small onion
- ¼ teaspoon each cinnamon, nutmeg and cumin
- ⅛ teaspoon cloves and ginger, salt and pepper
- 2½ tablespoons honey
- ¼ cup heavy cream

1. Cut squash in half and scoop seeds out. Put 1 tablespoon brown sugar and 1 tablespoon butter in each squash, turn skin side up onto sheet pan (2 large), pour enough stock to cover pan. Place cut potatoes, carrots and onions in pan with squash. Roast until squash is fork tender.

2. Take squash out of oven to cool. When cool enough to handle, scoop squash into stock pot and add vegetables in the stock pot as well. Cover with stock, add cinnamon, nutmeg, cumin, cloves, ginger, salt, pepper and honey.

3. Cook for 30 minutes or until vegetables are soft. Purée in a blender with a little heavy cream and more stock until desired consistency is met—optimally, smooth and creamy, not too thick.

KALAMATA-FIG TAPENADE

MAKES ½ CUP

- ½ cup dried black mission figs, stems trimmed and halved
- ¼ cup Port wine
- 1 cup Kalamata olives, pits removed and drained
- 1 tablespoon capers, drained
- 1 teaspoon garlic, chopped
- 1 tablespoon red wine vinegar
- ¼ teaspoon dried oregano
- 2 tablespoons olive oil

1. In a medium-sized bowl, soak figs with Port for 20 minutes.

2. Add Kalamata olives, capers, garlic, red wine vinegar, oregano and olive oil.

3. Purée in a food processor, pulsing for several minutes until combined. Tapenade should be slightly chunky so that olives still have some form. Serve with Grilled Foccacia (see recipe page 135).

WHITE BEAN ROASTED GARLIC DIP

MAKES 1 ½ CUPS

1 medium-sized head of garlic

1 teaspoon olive oil

1 (15-ounce) can of white beans, rinsed and drained

¾ teaspoon fresh rosemary, finely chopped

1 tablespoon fresh lemon juice

3 teaspoons blood orange avocado oil (available at Gourmet Cellar or other specialty shops)

3 tablespoons olive oil

salt and pepper to taste

1. Preheat oven to 400 degrees.

2. Place head of garlic onto a sheet of aluminum foil. Drizzle garlic with 1 teaspoon olive oil and wrap in foil. Roast in the oven for approximately 30 minutes or until garlic is soft. Allow to cool slightly.

3. Place white beans in a food processor. Cut roasted garlic in half and squeeze the inside into food processor, avoiding the skin. Add rosemary, lemon juice, both oils, salt and pepper. Purée until it is a smooth consistency, scraping sides of food processor every so often. Serve with Grilled Foccacia (see recipe page 135).

CUMIN-SPICED CARROT DIP

MAKES 2 CUPS

8 small to medium-sized carrots, quartered

¼ teaspoon coriander

½ teaspoon each, ground ginger and ground cumin

1 teaspoon chili garlic sauce

2¼ tablespoons honey

3 tablespoons olive oil

2 tablespoons red wine vinegar

salt and pepper to taste

1. In a small pot, cover carrots with water and bring to a boil. Cook for 25–30 minutes or until carrots are soft. Drain carrots.

2. In a food processor, combine cooked carrots with coriander, ginger, cumin, chili garlic sauce, honey, olive oil, red wine vinegar.

3. Purée until a smooth consistency. Season to taste with salt and pepper. Serve with Grilled Foccacia (see recipe page 135).

GRILLED FOCCACIA

SERVES 12–15

3 cups water

14 ounces flour

1 tablespoon salt

1 tablespoon yeast

2 teaspoons sugar

⅓ cup, plus 2 tablespoons olive oil

½ cup Parmesan cheese, shredded

2 tablespoons sea salt flakes

2 tablespoons fresh rosemary (optional), coarsely chopped

1. In the bowl of a stand mixer, using the dough hook attachment, combine water, flour and salt. Mix for 1–2 minutes or until well combined. Remove dough hook, cover the bowl and let sit for 20 minutes.

2. Sprinkle sugar and yeast over the top of dough, attach dough hook and mix 4–5 minutes until gluten forms and dough pulls slightly away from sides of bowl.

3. Transfer to an 18x13-inch sheet pan. With olive oil spread over the bottom of pan, spray dough with vegetable spray and lightly cover with plastic wrap. Let rest for 20 minutes.

4. Punch dough and repeat Step 2.

5. Let dough sit covered 20 more minutes before pulling dough to edges of pan. Using fingertips, poke holes on the surface to distribute dough. Cover dough and let rise for 45 minutes. Top with sea salt flakes, shredded Parmesan cheese and optional rosemary.

6. Bake at 425 degrees until golden brown, about 15–20 minutes.

7. Prepare outdoor grill.

8. After bread cools, cut into 2-inch slices. Drizzle with remaining 2 tablespoons olive oil, salt and pepper. Over medium heat, grill bread slices just enough to toast lightly on each side.

GRILLED VEGETABLE AND ITALIAN SAUSAGE LASAGNA

SERVES 10–11

- 1 cup All-Purpose Tomato Sauce (Recipe follows)
- 12 boiled lasagna noodles
- 1 lb. ground Italian sausage, cooked
- ¾ lb. Mustang Grilled Vegetables (See recipe page 66)
- 2 cups cooked spinach (or use frozen), drained
- 4 cups mozzarella, shredded
- 2 cups Parmesan, shredded
- 2 Roma tomatoes, cut into 8 slices
- 1 teaspoon dried Italian seasoning
- 2 tablespoons flat leaf parsley, chopped
- 3 tablespoons feta or goat cheese
- salt and pepper to taste

1. Preheat 350-degree oven.

2. In a 9x13-inch pan, pour 1 cup All-Purpose Tomato Sauce on the bottom of the pan. Place three lasagna noodles on top of sauce, then cooked sausage. Top with 1 cup mozzarella and ½ cup Parmesan.

3. Repeat with a second layer: 1 cup of All-Purpose Sauce, pasta, spinach, 1 cup of mozzarella and ½ cup Parmesan.

4. Repeat with a third layer: 1 cup of All-Purpose Sauce, pasta, Grilled Vegetables, 1 cup of mozzarella and ½ cup Parmesan.

5. Finally, cover with the last lasagna noodles and the last cup of All-Purpose Tomato Sauce, top with the remaining mozzarella and Parmesan. Top with the 8 slices of Roma tomatoes, parsley, Italian seasoning, feta cheese and salt and pepper.

6. Bake lasagna for 30–35 minutes or until cheese starts to brown.

ALL-PURPOSE TOMATO SAUCE

MAKES 12 CUPS

- 12 cups canned diced tomatoes
- 1 cup olive oil
- 3 tablespoons garlic, chopped

1. Purée diced tomatoes in blender for 10 seconds.

2. In a sauté pan add olive oil and garlic. Cook on medium-high heat until sizzling.

3. Add puréed tomatoes and simmer on stove for about 10 minutes.

4. Freeze remaining sauce up to two months.

MEET ME AT MUSTANG

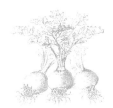

Menu

Chicken Noodle Soup

Tomato Bisque

Grilled Chicken Sausages
with Apples, Yams and Onions

Four Cheese Pasta

Bolognese Sauce

Montana Meatloaf

Lobster Pot Pie

Molasses Cookies

Oatmeal Raisin Cookies

Peanut Butter Cookies

Snickerdoodles

Chocolate Chip Cookies

The Shop

Throughout the year our regular customers come into the shop for meals to take home. We post our weekly menu on the website to make the planning easier. It's part of my mission at Mustang to make people's lives a little simpler by doing the cooking and helping them spend more time with family and friends, whether at a special dinner or a sledding party.

For some folks, like Jacqueline and David Boreham, Mustang dinners have become an annual tradition. Every December they order a batch of Lobster Pot Pies for a holiday dinner with their boys, Alexander and Jackson. It's a special occasion that marks a moment I look forward to each year. I love the way our food is part of people's lives. As with all of our regulars, I am thankful to see the faces of the Mustang friends who come and go each day, each week, year after year. That's a recipe for success.

Thermoses full of chicken noodle soup. Carole Sullivan sends the Boreham family home with their Lobster Pot Pies. The Mustang tower of salads. Four Cheese Pasta. Lunch at Mustang!

· · · · Grilled Chicken Sausages with Apples, Yams and Onions. Daily baked goods for your sweet tooth. Lobster Pot Pies. Gathering at the Mustang café.

CHICKEN NOODLE SOUP

SERVES 10–12

- 1 cup onion, diced
- 1 cup carrot, peeled and diced
- 1 cup celery, diced
- 1 tablespoon Canola oil
- 12 cups chicken stock
- 4 cups chicken, cooked and shredded (Costco's roasted chicken works great)
- 2 tablespoons flat leaf parsley, chopped
- salt & pepper
- 4 cups egg noodles, cooked

1. Sauté onions, carrots and celery in vegetable (or Canola) oil. Stir often and cook for about 10 minutes over medium heat.

2. Add chicken stock, bring to a low boil and cook for 10 more minutes.

3. Stir in shredded chicken and parsley.

4. Season with salt and pepper to desired taste.

5. Before serving, add egg noodles.

TOMATO BISQUE

SERVES 6–8

- 1 tablespoon butter
- 1 small onion, diced
- 2 (28-ounce) cans of diced tomatoes
- 3 tablespoons brown sugar
- 1 bay leaf
- 1 tablespoon dried basil
- ½ teaspoon ground cloves
- ½ cup heavy cream
- salt and pepper to taste

1. Melt butter in pot and add onions.

2. Let onions cook until soft and translucent.

3. Add tomatoes with their juices, then put in the brown sugar, bay leaf, basil and cloves.

4. Stir and bring to a boil. Turn to a simmer and let cook for 15–20 minutes.

5. Allow to cool slightly, then purée in a blender along with cream until smooth.

6. Add salt and pepper and serve.

GRILLED CHICKEN SAUSAGES WITH APPLES, YAMS AND ONIONS

SERVES 5–6

- ½ cup of butter
- 1 medium yellow onion, sliced 1 inch thick along the grain
- 4 heaping cups of yams, peeled and sliced ¼ inch thick
- 2 large green apples (Granny Smith), deseeded and sliced thick
- ½ cup of honey
- 5 Aidells Chicken Apple Sausages, marked on the grill

1. Melt the butter in a large sauté pan over low heat. When butter is melted, add the onions, stirring to break up sections for about 1 minute. Add yam slices and stir to evenly distribute in pan.

2. Cover the pan lightly with foil and stir occasionally until the yams are fork tender and slightly browned, about 15–20 minutes.

3. Add the apple slices and honey, stir and let cook about 5 minutes.

4. Slice grilled chicken sausages into 5–6 sections on the bias, and add to the pan. Stir and let cook until sausages are warmed through. Serve family-style on a large platter.

FOUR CHEESE PASTA

SERVES 6–8

- 1 lb. penne pasta
- 1 quart milk
- 8 tablespoons unsalted butter
- ½ cup all-purpose flour
- 2 cups pepper Jack, grated
- 2 cups sharp Cheddar, grated
- 1 cup Jarlsberg, grated
- 4 ounces Brie, peeled and cut into chunks
- ½ teaspoon black pepper
- ½ teaspoon salt
- ½ teaspoon ground nutmeg
- 1 cup breadcrumbs
- 2 tablespoons butter, melted

1. Preheat oven to 375 degrees F.

2. Cook pasta according to instructions.

3. Heat milk in a small saucepan, but don't boil it. Melt 8 tablespoons butter in a large saucepan and add the flour, whisking over low heat for 2 minutes. While whisking, slowly add the hot milk and cook for a minute or two more until thickened and smooth. Remove from heat, add the cheese, salt, pepper and nutmeg. Add the cooked macaroni and stir well. Pour into a 3-quart baking dish.

4. Melt the remaining butter, mix with the breadcrumbs and sprinkle on top. Bake for 12–15 minutes or until the sauce is bubbly and the macaroni is browned on the top.

BOLOGNESE SAUCE

SERVES 6–8

- 1 medium yellow onion, chopped
- 2 carrots, peeled and chopped
- 2 celery stalks, minced
- 4 tablespoons of olive oil
- 1 lb. ground beef
- 1 lb. Italian sausage
- 1 cup white wine
- 5¾ cups diced canned tomatoes (with juice)
- 2 cups chicken stock
- 2 cups heavy cream
- ⅓ cup parsley, chopped
- ½ cup Parmesan cheese, finely grated

1. In a large pan sauté onion, carrots, celery in olive oil, about 10 minutes.

2. Add ground beef and Italian sausage, cook on medium heat, breaking up clumps of meat until traces of red are gone.

3. Add white wine, raise the heat a bit and cook, stirring occasionally until most of the liquid is evaporated.

4. In a separate bowl, crush diced tomatoes (with juice). Add them to the pot and then add chicken stock. Cook for an hour or so, then season with salt and pepper.

5. Add heavy cream and cook for another 15–20 minutes.

6. Finish with chopped parsley. Serve over cooked spaghetti and garnish with Parmesan cheese.

MONTANA MEATLOAF

SERVES 8

- 2 lbs. local Montana grass-fed ground beef
- 1 lb. Italian sausage blended together
- ½ cup carrot, shredded
- ½ cup parsley, chopped
- 1 large shallot, diced
- ½ cup oatmeal soaked in ⅓ cup milk for 5 minutes
- 2 eggs
- ½ teaspoon nutmeg
- 3 teaspoons Pickapeppa Sauce
- 2 teaspoons Worcestershire Sauce
- 4 dashes of Tabasco
- 1 teaspoon salt
- ½ teaspoon pepper

1. Mix ingredients together, place in 8x12-inch casserole pan and top with four pieces of pepper bacon.

2. Bake in 375-degree oven for approximately 40 minutes or until bacon is browned and center of meatloaf springs back just slightly when pressed down.

LOBSTER POT PIE

SERVES 6–8

1 small yellow onion, chopped

½ cup fennel, chopped

1 cup carrots, peeled, diced and par-boiled

½ cup butter

½ cup flour

4 cups fish stock or clam juice

1 tablespoon Pernod

1½ teaspoons kosher salt

½ teaspoon fresh ground black pepper

3 tablespoons heavy cream

1 lb. lobster meat (cooked)

1 cup frozen peas

1 cup frozen pearl onions

¼ cup flat leaf parsley, chopped

1 tablespoon tarragon, chopped

1 tablespoon heavy cream

½ Torte Dough (See recipe page 74)

FILLING

1. Sauté onions and fennel in butter for 10–15 minutes.

2. Add the flour and cook for 3 more minutes stirring occasionally. Slowly add the stock, whisking constantly, then add the Pernod, salt and pepper. Simmer for 5 more minutes. Add the heavy cream.

3. Cut the lobster meat into medium-sized cubes. Place the lobster, peas, carrots, onions, parsley and tarragon in a bowl.

4. Pour the sauce over the lobster mixture and adjust seasonings to taste. Season with salt and pepper to taste. Set aside.

POT PIE

1. Preheat oven to 425 degrees.

2. Divide the dough in half and roll out to fit a 9x13-inch lightly buttered casserole pan. You will only need half the dough so freeze the rest.

3. Divide remaining dough in half again. Place one crust in the dish and fill with the lobster mixture. Top with second crust. Crimp the crusts together. Brush top of crust with heavy cream. Make a few slashes in dough to vent.

4. Bake for approximately 20 minutes or until crust is golden brown and filling is bubbling.

5. Remove from oven and allow to sit for 5–10 minutes before serving with a light green salad.

MOLASSES COOKIES

MAKES 3 DOZEN

2½ cups unsalted butter, softened

1½ cups dark brown sugar

1½ cups granulated sugar

1 cup molasses

3 eggs

1 tablespoon vanilla extract

7 cups all-purpose flour

2 tablespoons baking soda

1½ teaspoons salt

1½ tablespoons ground cinnamon

1 tablespoon ground ginger

2¼ teaspoons ground cloves

¾ teaspoon allspice

1. In an electric stand mixer with the paddle attachment, cream butter and sugars. Add molasses and mix well. Add vanilla, then add eggs one at a time, scraping down bowl after each egg is incorporated.

2. In a separate bowl, mix the dry ingredients with a whisk.

3. While mixer is running on low, slowly add dry ingredients to wet ingredients. Mix until completely combined.

4. Preheat oven to 375 degrees.

5. Scoop dough (I use a commercial-size 1⅝-ounce scoop) and press lightly onto a parchment-lined sheet pan. Chill in refrigerator for 15–20 minutes until dough feels firm to the touch.

6. Bake for 8 minutes, rotate and bake for another 8 minutes.

Chilling the dough just for 15-20 minutes before baking ensures that all the cookies are uniform.

OATMEAL RAISIN COOKIES

MAKES 3 DOZEN

- 1½ cups unsalted butter, softened
- 1½ cups light brown sugar
- ¾ cup granulated sugar
- 3 eggs
- 1½ teaspoons vanilla extract
- 2¼ cups all-purpose flour
- 1½ teaspoons baking soda
- 1½ teaspoons cinnamon
- ¾ teaspoon salt
- 4½ cups old-fashioned oats
- 1½ cups raisins

1. In a stand mixer with a paddle attachment, cream butter and sugars well. Add vanilla, then add eggs one at a time, scraping down the bowl after each egg is incorporated.

2. In a separate mixing bowl, combine dry ingredients with a whisk.

3. Add the dry ingredients to the wet ingredients and then add the oats and raisins. Mix until completely combined.

4. Preheat oven at 375 degrees.

5. Scoop dough (I use a commercial-size 1⅝-ounce scoop) and press lightly onto a parchment-lined sheet pan. Chill in refrigerator for 15–20 minutes until dough feels firm to the touch.

7. Bake for 8 minutes, rotate the pan and then bake for another 8 minutes.

Peanut Butter Cookies

MAKES 3 DOZEN

- 1½ cups unsalted butter, softened
- 1½ cups smooth peanut butter
- 1½ cups light brown sugar
- 1½ cups granulated sugar
- 3 eggs
- 1 tablespoon vanilla
- 3¾ cups all-purpose flour
- ¾ teaspoon baking soda
- ¾ teaspoon baking powder
- ¾ teaspoon salt
- 2 handfuls of roasted peanuts, chopped

1. In a stand mixer with a paddle attachment, cream butter and peanut butter until combined. Add sugars and cream well. Add vanilla, then add eggs one at a time, scraping down bowl after each egg is incorporated.

2. In a separate mixing bowl, combine dry ingredients with a whisk.

3. Add dry ingredients to wet ingredients and then add peanuts; mix until completely combined.

4. Preheat oven to 375 degrees.

5. Scoop dough (I use a commercial-size 1⅝-ounce scoop) and press lightly with a fork in criss-cross pattern onto a parchment lined sheet pan.

6. Refrigerate dough for 15–20 minutes until dough feels firm to the touch.

7. Bake for 8 minutes, rotate and bake for another 8 minutes.

SNICKERDOODLES

MAKES 2 ½ DOZEN

- 2 cups unsalted butter, softened
- 3 cups granulated sugar
- 4 eggs
- 6 cups all-purpose flour
- 4 teaspoons cream of tartar
- 2 teaspoons baking soda
- ½ teaspoon salt

1. In a stand mixer with a paddle attachment, cream butter and sugar well. Add eggs one at a time, scraping down bowl after each egg is incorporated.

2. In a separate mixing bowl, combine dry ingredients and mix with a whisk. Add dry ingredients to wet ingredients until completely combined.

3. Refrigerate dough for 15–20 minutes until dough feels firm to the touch.

4. Preheat oven to 375 degrees.

5. When chilled, scoop desired size (I use a commercial-size $1\frac{5}{8}$-ounce scoop), roll in cinnamon and sugar mix and bake on parchment-paper-lined sheet pan for 8 minutes. Rotate pan and bake for another 8 minutes. Allow to cool and remove from rack.

CHOCOLATE CHIP COOKIES

MAKES 2 ½ DOZEN

- 2 cups unsalted butter, softened
- 1 ½ cups light brown sugar
- 1 cup granulated sugar
- 4 teaspoons vanilla
- 2 eggs
- 4 ½ cups all-purpose flour
- 1 teaspoon salt
- 2 teaspoons baking soda
- 4 cups semi-sweet chocolate chips

1. Preheat oven to 375 degrees.

2. Cream butter and sugar well in the bowl of an electric mixer. Add vanilla and then add the eggs one at a time.

3. In a separate bowl, combine the dry ingredients with a whisk. Add the dry ingredients to the wet ingredients to combine and then add chocolate chips until completely incorporated evenly.

4. Scoop dough (I use a commercial-size $1\frac{5}{8}$-ounce scoop) and press lightly onto a parchment-lined sheet pan.

5. Chill in refrigerator for 15–20 minutes until dough feels firm to the touch.

6. Bake for 8 minutes, rotate and bake for another 8 minutes.

INDEX